Frommer's

San Diego
day BY day®

2nd Edition

by Mark Hiss

WILEY
Wiley Publishing, Inc.

S0-ASF-324

Contents

Published by:

Wiley Publishing, Inc.

111 River St.
Hoboken, NJ 07030-5774

ISBN 978-0-470-89072-1 (paper); ISBN 978-1-118-01507-0 (ebk);
ISBN 978-1-118-01508-7 (ebk); ISBN 978-1-118-01509-4 (ebk)

Editor: Alexia Travaglini
Production Editor: Lindsay Conner
Photo Editor: Richard Fox
Cartographer: Andrew Dolan
Production by Wiley Indianapolis Composition Services

Front cover photos, left to right: © Adam Jones / Danita Delmont.com / Alamy Images; © Russ Bishop / Alamy Images; © Kevin Schafer / Getty Images

Back cover photo: © Brett Shoaf / Artistic Visuals

For information on our other products and services or to obtain technical support, please contact our Customer Care Department within the U.S. at 877/762-2974, outside the U.S. at 317/572-3993 or fax 317/572-4002.

Wiley also publishes its books in a variety of electronic formats. Some content that appears in print may not be available in electronic formats.

Manufactured in China

5 4 3 2 1

A Note from the Editorial Director

Organizing your time. That's what this guide is all about.

Other guides give you long lists of things to see and do and then expect you to fit the pieces together. The *Day by Day* guides are different. These guides tell you the best of everything, and then they show you how to see it *in the smartest, most time-efficient way*. Our authors have designed detailed itineraries organized by time, neighborhood, or special interest. And each tour comes with a bulleted map that takes you from stop to stop.

Hoping to loll on a beach in San Diego's year-round perfect weather? Sample fish tacos or visit the giant pandas at one of the nation's finest zoos? How about strolling through Old Town, the cradle of modern California, or the Gaslamp Quarter, where San Diego's urban revival began? Whatever your interest or schedule, the Day by Days give you the smartest routes to follow. Not only do we take you to the top attractions, hotels, and restaurants, but we also help you access those special moments that locals get to experience—those "finds" that turn tourists into travelers.

The Day by Days are also your top choice if you're looking for one complete guide for all your travel needs. The best hotels and restaurants for every budget, the greatest shopping values, the wildest nightlife—it's all here.

Why should you trust our judgment? Because our authors personally visit each place they write about. They're an independent lot who say what they think and would never include places they wouldn't recommend to their best friends. They're also open to suggestions from readers. If you'd like to contact them, please send your comments our way at feedback@frommers.com, and we'll pass them on.

Enjoy your Day by Day guide—the most helpful travel companion you can buy. And have the trip of a lifetime.

Warm regards,

Kelly Regan

Kelly Regan, Editorial Director
Frommer's Travel Guides

About the Author

Mark Hiss is a third-generation Southern Californian who has spent more than 25 years in San Diego. He was founding editor of both the visitor guide *Where San Diego* and *Performances*, the playbill magazine for the city's leading performing arts venues. He is also author of *Frommer's San Diego*, coauthor of *Frommer's California Day by Day*, and a contributor to *Frommer's California*. In a previous life he was a publicist who worked for several San Diego theater companies.

An Additional Note

Please be advised that travel information is subject to change at any time—and this is especially true of prices. We therefore suggest that you write or call ahead for confirmation when making your travel plans. The authors, editors, and publisher cannot be held responsible for the experiences of readers while traveling. Your safety is important to us, however, so we encourage you to stay alert and be aware of your surroundings.

Star Ratings, Icons & Abbreviations

Every hotel, restaurant, and attraction listing in this guide has been ranked for quality, value, service, amenities, and special features using a **star-rating system.** Hotels, restaurants, attractions, shopping, and nightlife are rated on a scale of zero stars (recommended) to three stars (exceptional). In addition to the star-rating system, we also use a **kids icon** to point out the best bets for families. Within each tour, we recommend cafes, bars, or restaurants where you can take a break. Each of these stops appears in a shaded box marked with a coffee-cup-shaped bullet ☕.

The following **abbreviations** are used for credit cards:

AE	American Express	DISC	Discover	V	Visa
DC	Diners Club	MC	MasterCard		

Travel Resources at Frommers.com

Frommer's travel resources don't end with this guide. Frommer's website, **www.frommers.com,** has travel information on more than 4,000 destinations. We update features regularly, giving you access to the most current trip-planning information and the best airfare, lodging, and car-rental bargains. You can also listen to podcasts, connect with other Frommers.com members through our active-reader forums, share your travel photos, read blogs from guidebook editors and fellow travelers, and much more.

A Note on Prices

In the "Take a Break" and "Best Bets" sections of this book, we have used a system of dollar signs to show a range of costs for 1 night in a hotel (the price of a double-occupancy room) or the cost of an entree at a restaurant. Use the following table to decipher the dollar signs:

Cost	Hotels	Restaurants
$	under $100	under $10
$$	$100–$200	$10–$20
$$$	$200–$300	$20–$30
$$$$	$300–$400	$30–$40
$$$$$	over $400	over $40

An Invitation to the Reader

In researching this book, we discovered many wonderful places—hotels, restaurants, shops, and more. We're sure you'll find others. Please tell us about them, so we can share the information with your fellow travelers in upcoming editions. If you were disappointed with a recommendation, we'd love to know that, too. Please write to:

Frommer's San Diego Day by Day, 2nd Edition
Wiley Publishing, Inc. • 111 River St. • Hoboken, NJ 07030-5774

18 Favorite **Moments**

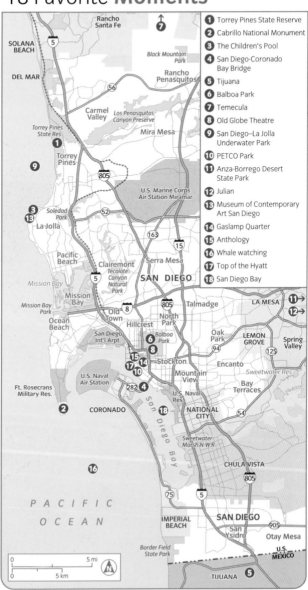

1. Torrey Pines State Reserve
2. Cabrillo National Monument
3. The Children's Pool
4. San Diego-Coronado Bay Bridge
5. Tijuana
6. Balboa Park
7. Temecula
8. Old Globe Theatre
9. San Diego–La Jolla Underwater Park
10. PETCO Park
11. Anza-Borrego Desert State Park
12. Julian
13. Museum of Contemporary Art San Diego
14. Gaslamp Quarter
15. Anthology
16. Whale watching
17. Top of the Hyatt
18. San Diego Bay

Previous page: Catching some waves in La Jolla.

I f you think San Diego is just about wiggling your toes in the sand or cooing over cuddly panda bears, think again. Combining big-city style with small-town heart, this seaside destination offers an embarrassment of riches: stunning natural beauty, high-octane nightlife, world-class cultural organizations, family-friendly attractions, and sophisticated dining. Oh, did I mention it has the country's best weather as well? San Diego is also perched on the world's busiest international border, with the sights, sounds, and tastes of Mexico just a Chihuahua's length away.

1 Escaping to Torrey Pines State Reserve. Dramatically set atop 300-foot (91m) cliffs overlooking the Pacific, this reserve is home to the rarest pine tree in North America. Short trails crisscross the delicate landscape, which also incorporates one of San Diego's best beaches. *See p 97.*

2 Taking in the city's best panorama. Cabrillo National Monument not only offers a whirlwind history tour, beginning with San Diego's European discovery in 1542, it also provides unsurpassed 360-degree views of downtown and beyond. From its location at the tip of Point Loma—and at 422 feet (129m) above sea level—it's also a great vantage point from which to watch migrating Pacific gray whales in the winter. *See p 88.*

Old Point Loma lighthouse at Cabrillo National Monument.

3 Communing with seals and sea lions. The Children's Pool, a picturesque cove in La Jolla, was named for the toddlers who could

Torrey Pines State Natural Reserve.

safely frolic behind its protective, man-made sea wall. A colony of pinnipeds came to like it equally, and now the beach is shared—sometimes a little uneasily—between humans and seals. *See p 60.*

❹ **Zipping across the San Diego–Coronado Bay Bridge.** Roll down the windows, put the top down, and let the wind blow through your hair as you cruise along this graceful engineering marvel. It's always a bit of a rush, and the views are spectacular, so try to keep your eyes on the road. *See p 67.*

❺ **Making a run for the border.** What a difference a line makes. Once you cross it, you're instantly immersed in the chaotic vibrancy of Mexico's fourth-largest city. Just a 20-minute drive from downtown, Tijuana has a raucous tourist zone with plentiful shopping, as well as an array of cultural and culinary delights. *See p 154.*

❻ **Spending an idyllic day in Balboa Park.** This is one of the world's great urban cultural parks, home to more than a dozen of the city's top museums. There are dazzling gardens, glorious Spanish Colonial Revival architecture, and the world-famous San Diego Zoo as well. Balboa Park is San Diego's crown jewel. *See p 9.*

❼ **Toasting the good life.** Just across the county line in Temecula, about 60 miles (97km) north of downtown San Diego, are some two-dozen wineries. They range from mom-and-pop operations with minimal amenities to slick commercial ventures with fancy tasting rooms, retail boutiques, and restaurants. Cheers. *See p 149.*

❽ **Being a groundling.** You won't have to stand like they did in William Shakespeare's day, but you can see the Bard's works alfresco at the Old Globe Theatre's summer

Juan Rodriguez Cabrillo statue.

Shakespeare Festival. The Tony Award–winning Old Globe performs Shakespeare's work in true repertory style, alternating three different productions at its open-air theater. *See p 21.*

⑨ Paddling with the fishes. The calm surfaces and clear waters of the San Diego–La Jolla Underwater Park are the ultimate local spot for a little kayaking. This ecological reserve features sea caves and vibrant marine life, including California's state marine fish, the electric-orange garibaldi. *See p 60.*

⑩ Buying some peanuts and Cracker Jacks. San Diego's Major League Baseball team, the Padres, play at PETCO Park, a state-of-the-art ballpark that opened in 2004. Incorporating seven buildings that date as far back as 1909, PETCO's clever design and downtown location have made it a fan favorite. *See p 129.*

⑪ Witnessing the desert's spring fling. For a period of several weeks—usually late February through March—Anza-Borrego Desert State Park magically comes alive with a carpet of blooming wildflowers. A brilliant palette of pink, lavender, red, orange, and yellow transforms the rugged landscape into a colorful oasis. *See p 98.*

⑫ Getting in touch with your pioneer spirit. The mountain hamlet of Julian was founded as a gold-mining town in the 1860s, but it gained fame for another mother lode: apples. Today, this rustic community has a distinctly Victorian, Old West charm, redolent of hot apple pies. *See p 150.*

⑬ Challenging your perception. The city's most important museum is the Museum of Contemporary Art San Diego (MCASD). With a flagship space in La Jolla and two downtown annexes, this internationally

Sea lions lolling on the beach at the Children's Pool in La Jolla.

prominent museum offers ongoing exhibitions of cutting-edge art, as well as a roster of special events. A visit to any of MCASD's facilities is guaranteed to be a thought-provoking experience. *See p 57.*

⑭ Strolling the Gaslamp Quarter. For dining, shopping, dancing, drinking, or just soaking up some local flavor, this is the place to be. People-watching opportunities abound—if you can manage to take your eyes off the exquisitely restored Victorian commercial buildings in this 16½-block district. *See p 10.*

⑮ Eating to the beat. Architecturally smashing, culinarily superb, and musically sophisticated, Anthology is a fine-dining restaurant masquerading as an acoustically excellent concert venue. Or is it the other way around? Anthology hosts top-name jazz, world music, blues, and rock artists, and you don't have to eat

Alcazar Garden, Balboa Park.

dinner to see the show (but you'd miss out on half the fun). *See p 121.*

16 Scouting for whales. Every year, from December through March, Pacific gray whales pass through San Diego waters, making their way to and from breeding lagoons in Mexico. There are ample opportunities to observe these gentle giants from both land and sea as they undertake one of the longest migrations of any mammal. *See p 32.*

17 Watching for the green flash. There's no better place to watch for the storied "green flash"—which occurs when the sun sinks beneath the horizon—than the Top of the Hyatt. This luxe lounge is located 40 stories above the Embarcadero in the West Coast's tallest waterfront building. *See p 118.*

18 Cruising the bay. Whether it's a weekend-brunch sightseeing tour, a chartered sailboat excursion, or just a water-taxi ride to Coronado, don't miss an opportunity to spend some time on San Diego Bay. Spanish conquistador Sebastián Vizcaíno described it in 1602 as "a port which must be the best to be found in all the South Sea." Discover it for yourself. *See the Embarcadero Neighborhood tour on p 54.* ●

Bar goers at Balboa Park.

The Best in **One Day**

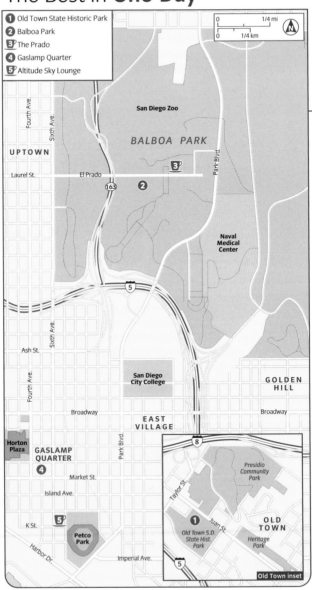

1 Old Town State Historic Park
2 Balboa Park
3 The Prado
4 Gaslamp Quarter
5 Altitude Sky Lounge

0 ——— 1/4 mi
0 ——— 1/4 km

San Diego Zoo

BALBOA PARK

UPTOWN

Fourth Ave.

Sixth Ave.

Laurel St.   El Prado

163

Park Blvd.

Naval
Medical
Center

5

Ash St.

Sixth Ave.

Fourth Ave.

San Diego
City College

GOLDEN
HILL

Broadway   Broadway

EAST
VILLAGE

Park Blvd.

Horton
Plaza

GASLAMP
QUARTER
4

Market St.

Island Ave.

K St.   5

Petco
Park

Harbor Dr.

Imperial Ave.

8

Taylor St.

Presidio
Community
Park

Juan St.

OLD
TOWN

1

Old Town S.D.
State Hist.
Park

Heritage
Park

5

Old Town inset

Previous page: A proud resident of the San Diego Zoo.

I f you have only 24 hours in San Diego, you may be tempted to blow the whole day on the beach or at the zoo. While it's hard to argue with that approach, it would deprive you of experiencing San Diego's robust and unusual heritage as the birthplace of California, with deep ties to Spain, Mexico, Wild West history, and the U.S. military. Besides, you'll still get plenty of sun as you tour through Old Town, and you just might hear the animals squawk and roar from the zoo as you explore Balboa Park next door. START: **Blue or Green Line trolley to Old Town Transit Center.**

1 ★ **Old Town State Historic Park.** Dedicated to re-creating the early life of the city from 1821 to 1872, this is where San Diego's Mexican heritage is best celebrated. It's California's most-visited state park, featuring 20 structures (some original, some reconstructed), including the home of a wealthy family, from around 1872, and the fledgling town's one-room schoolhouse. Memorabilia and exhibits are on view in some buildings; visitor-oriented shops and restaurants are incorporated into the rest. On Wednesdays and Saturdays, from 10am to 4pm, costumed park volunteers reenact life in the 1800s with cooking and crafts demonstrations, a working blacksmith, and parlor singing; there's storytelling on the

green Tuesdays and Thursdays, noon to 2pm, and Friday from 1 to 3pm. Free 1-hour walking tours leave daily at 11am and 2pm from the Robinson-Rose House. ⏱ *At least 1 hr. The park is bordered by Juan, Congress, Twiggs, and Wallace sts.* ☎ *619/220-5422. www.parks. ca.gov. Free admission. Museums daily 10am–5pm, most restaurants till 9pm. Trolley: Blue or Green Line to Old Town.*

2 ★★★ **kids Balboa Park.** Like New York's Central Park and San Francisco's Golden Gate Park, the emerald in San Diego's crown is Balboa Park, a 1,174-acre (475 hectare) city-owned playground and the largest urban cultural park in the nation. The park's most distinctive features

Old Town State Historic Park.

Reflections at Balboa Park.

are its mature landscaping, the architectural beauty of the Spanish Colonial Revival–style buildings lining the pedestrian thoroughfare (byproducts of expositions in 1915 and 1935), and its 15 engaging and diverse museums. You'll also find eight different gardens, walkways, 4.5 miles (7km) of hiking trails in Florida Canyon, an ornate pavilion with the world's largest outdoor organ, an old-fashioned carousel, an IMAX domed theater, the acclaimed Old Globe Theatre, and the San Diego Zoo. ⏱ *At least 2 hr. (or more, depending on which museums pique your interest). Primary entrances are at Sixth Ave. and Laurel St. on the west side and Park Blvd. and Presidents Way on the east side.* ☎ *619/239-0512. www. balboapark.org. Museum prices vary; free organ concerts are presented every Sun at 2pm and Mon– Thurs at 7:30pm in summer; free as well as paid, self-guided tours are available from the Visitor Center, open daily 9:30am–4:30pm (extended hours in summer). Attraction hours vary, but many are 10am–5pm. Bus: 1, 3, 7, or 120; a free tram operates within the park, daily 8:30am–6pm (extended hours in summer).*

In ❸ **The Prado,** Balboa Park's sophisticated-but-casual Prado restaurant, is a great place to catch your breath and set a spell, whether you're stopping in for lunch, dinner, or just some drinks and appetizers. This sprawling restaurant complex in the baroque House of Hospitality has lovely patio dining (it overlooks a garden popular for weddings), a lounge where you can often find live entertainment, and special event spaces where wine tastings and cooking classes are held. *1549 El Prado.* ☎ *619/557-9441. www. cohnrestaurants.com. $11–$30.*

❹ ★★ **Gaslamp Quarter.** Where others had seen only dismal mud flats melting into a shallow bay, businessman Alonzo Horton saw untapped potential. In 1867 he undertook an audacious plan to lure citizens away from Old Town with the founding of "New Town," several miles to the south. New Town is now known as the Gaslamp Quarter, and it's become more successful than anything Alonzo could have hoped for. It's comprised of 16½ blocks of restored historic buildings housing dozens of restaurants, bars, clubs, and boutiques—this is where you'll find San Diego's most vigorous nightlife, fabulous Victorian architecture, and excellent people-watching. Begin your tour of the area at Horton Plaza shopping center, where you not only can shop and dine, but also catch a play or a movie. ⏱ *At least 1 hr. (not including dining or entertainment options). The district is bounded by Broadway on the north, L St. and the waterfront to the south, Fourth Ave. to the west, and Sixth Ave. to the east. Gaslamp Quarter Association* ☎ *619/233-5227. www. gaslamp.org. Mall stores tend to stay open till 9pm weekdays, 7 or 8pm on weekends; independent stores are generally open till 7 or 8pm Mon–Thurs, 8 or 9pm Fri–Sat, and 6 or 7pm Sun. Restaurants usually serve till 10pm Sun–Thurs, with longer hours Fri–Sat. Bars are usually open till 2am daily; most clubs are open till 2am Thurs–Sat. Crowds are thick Thurs–Sat and whenever there's a large convention in town or a baseball game at PETCO Park. Parking structures are available at Horton Plaza, Market St. and Sixth Ave., and Sixth Ave. and K St. Trolley: Orange Line. Bus: Any downtown route.*

Flamingos at the San Diego Zoo.

Finish off your day by rising above it all for a nightcap at the open-air ⑤ **Altitude Sky Lounge,** 22 floors up from the Gaslamp commotion. This long, narrow space is in the Gaslamp Quarter Marriott overlooking PETCO Park and the Convention Center. It offers fire pits, lounges, and DJ-spun grooves, as well as appetizers from the first-floor restaurant. As with many Gaslamp Quarter venues, lines begin forming around 10pm on weekends (or when the Padres are playing). *660 K St. (btw. Sixth and Seventh aves.).* ☎ *619/696-0234. www. altitudeskylounge.com. Daily 5pm–1:30am. $5–$12.*

The scene on the roof at Altitude Skybar.

The Best in **Two Days**

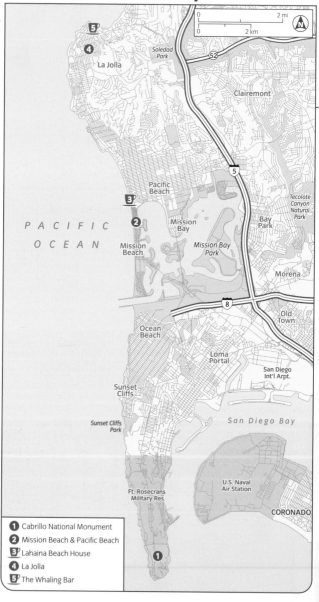

1 Cabrillo National Monument
2 Mission Beach & Pacific Beach
3 Lahaina Beach House
4 La Jolla
5 The Whaling Bar

You don't have to venture far for stunning natural settings in San Diego, which means it's easy to season your nature romps with a little history, great food, and even some shopping. This itinerary showcases the extremes of SoCal coastal living, from rollicking Pacific Beach to refined La Jolla. You'll really need your sunscreen today, though. A car is in order too. While it is possible to tackle this itinerary via public transportation, it's much more practical to have your own set of wheels. START: **Bus route 84 to Cabrillo National Monument.**

① ★★★ kids Cabrillo National Monument. Breathtaking views mingle with the early history of San Diego, specifically the arrival of Juan Rodríguez Cabrillo in 1542. His statue is prominently featured here, along with a historic lighthouse built in 1855, a small museum, the remnants of World War II artillery batteries, a visitor center with lots of books and souvenirs for sale, and a theater screening short videos about local natural history and the age of exploration. The park's setting 422 feet (129m) above sea level at the tip of Point Loma makes it a great vantage point for watching migrating Pacific gray whales December through March. National Park Service rangers also lead walks at the monument, and there are tide pools to explore at the base of the peninsula. The Bayside Trail is an easy hike (3.2 miles/5km round-trip) along an interpreted walkway that leads to a lookout over the bay. ⏱ *At least 1 hr. There are great picnicking spots here, but no food facilities, so pack a lunch. 1800 Cabrillo Memorial Dr.* ☎ *619/557-5450. www.nps.gov/cabr. Admission $5 per vehicle, $3 for walk-ins. Daily 9am–5pm. Bus: Route 84.*

② Mission Beach and Pacific Beach. This is it. Ground zero for the party hearty, freewheeling Southern California beach lifestyle. These two beaches form a 3-mile (5km) stretch of sand paralleled by a cement boardwalk that hosts a nonstop parade of surfers, skaters, bikers, joggers, and plain old beach lovers. South Mission Beach is where you'll find serious beach volleyball and a seaside basketball

Hiking the trails at Cabrillo National Monument.

The boardwalk at Mission Beach.

court. Farther north is Belmont Park, an amusement park whose star attraction is a 1925 wooden roller coaster. Another 1925 holdover is Crystal Pier at the foot of Garnet Avenue in Pacific Beach (or PB as it's known). This 400-foot-long (122m) wooden pier now supports rental cottages, but is open daily to the public, offering great views of the local surfers. The street-side action in these beach zones takes place primarily on Mission Boulevard (heading north from Belmont Park) and Garnet Avenue (running east from Mission Blvd.), both overflowing with restaurants, clubs, and retailers. Rent a bike and join the parade. ⏲ *At least 1 hr. (or more, depending on how much frolicking in the surf you want to do). Discover Pacific Beach:* ☎ *858/273-3303. www.pacificbeach.org. Bus: Route 8/9 from Old Town Transit Center.*

An old beach bungalow transformed into a simple, unpretentious, utterly rockin' eatery and bar, **3️⃣ Lahaina Beach House** has been a PB institution for a generation. Its weathered wooden deck, just inches from the boardwalk, is standing-room-only on sunny weekends, and provides a sensory overload of sights and sounds. The food is basic—omelets, burgers, fish tacos; the atmosphere is pure beach party. Cash only. *710 Oliver Ave. (along the boardwalk between Reed Ave. and Pacific Beach Dr.).* ☎ *858/270-3888. 8am–9pm. $7–$11.*

4️⃣ ★★★ La Jolla. About the only thing La Jolla shares in common with the beach communities to the south is the Pacific Ocean. Locals refer to La Jolla's principal shopping and dining

Surfing near Crystal Pier, Pacific Beach.

Seaside inspiration in La Jolla.

district as "the village," and it's one of the classiest villages you could imagine. High-end boutiques, antiques stores, art galleries, and fine restaurants line the streets; while just steps away, a dramatic coastline of sandstone cliffs and picturesque coves with tropical-blue waters awaits. And this beauty has brains, too—La Jolla is a center for local arts and culture, providing a home for the University of California, San Diego (where you'll find the Tony Award–winning La Jolla Playhouse and the Stuart Collection of site-specific art); the flagship space for the Museum of Contemporary Art San Diego; and the Athenaeum Music and Arts Library, which presents concerts and art exhibits. La Jolla is a Southern California Riviera. ⏱ *3 hr. (or more if you want to enjoy an exhibit or show).* www.lajollabythe sea.com. ☎ 858/454-5718. Bus: Route 30 from Mission Blvd. and Grand Ave. in PB.

La Valencia Hotel is the grande dame of La Jolla. The Pink Lady originally opened in 1926, and its Mediterranean style and killer location made it a favorite of Hollywood golden age celebs like Greta Garbo

and Charlie Chaplin. The hotel's clubby watering hole, **5 ★ The Whaling Bar,** became something of a West Coast Algonquin for literary types, as well as a popular spot for a second generation of movie stars brought in by La Jolla native Gregory Peck, who also cofounded the La Jolla Playhouse. Stop in for a drink and listen closely—you just might hear the walls talking. *1132 Prospect St. (at Herschel Ave.).* ☎ *858/551-3761 or 858/454-0771.* www.lavalencia.com. *11:30am–10pm. $5–$15.*

A kite runner on Pacific Beach.

The Best in **Three Days**

1. San Diego Zoo
2. Extraordinary Desserts
3. Embarcadero
4. Hotel del Coronado

Now that you have an overview of the city—from its Spanish colonial and Mexican-American frontier roots to its high-octane nightlife and lively, lovely beach communities—it's time to go where the wild things are. Put on a pair of comfortable shoes and head out to San Diego's best-known attraction, the San Diego Zoo. Then cap your day with a visit to the area's most iconic structure: the Hotel del Coronado. START: **Bus 7 to the San Diego Zoo.**

1 ★★★ kids **San Diego Zoo.** "World famous" often precedes any mention of the San Diego Zoo, and for good reason. Established in 1916, the zoo was a pioneer in developing naturalistic, humane enclosures. It's also a global leader in endangered species preservation with its breeding programs. The zoo's most recent addition is Elephant Odyssey, featuring a herd of Asian elephants, as well as life-size replicas of prehistoric animals that roamed the San Diego region. Other highlights include giant pandas (this is one of only four zoos in the country with pandas in residence);

Elephant Odyssey, San Diego Zoo.

Monkey Trails and Forest Tales, the zoo's largest, most elaborate habitat, re-creating a wooded forest filled with a variety of rare creatures; Gorilla Tropics, housing two troops of lowland gorillas; and Ituri Forest, which simulates an African rainforest (complete with hippos viewed from underwater via a wall of glass). ⏲ *At least 3 hr. 2920 Zoo Dr.* ☎ *619/234-3153 (recorded info), or 619/231-1515. www.sandiegozoo. org. Admission $37 adults, $27 children 3–11, free for active-duty military (U.S. and foreign); discounted 2-day passes can be used for both the zoo and Wild Animal Park. Sept to mid-June daily 9am–4pm (grounds close at 5 or 6pm); mid-June to Aug daily 9am–8pm (grounds close at 9pm). Bus: 7.*

You've earned this one. After all the walking you've done, even the most demanding diet plan will surely allow for a sinful creation from **2** ★★★ **Extraordinary Desserts.** Set in an architecturally striking space, this local standout also serves panini, salads, and artisan cheeses, as well as wine and beer. Chef/proprietor Karen Krasne sells her own line of jams, confections, and syrups, too, if you want to take a taste of San Diego home. *Bus 7 to Broadway and Union St., walk 4 blocks north to 1430 Union St.* ☎ *619/ 294-7001. www.extraordinary desserts.com. Mon–Thurs 8:30am– 11pm; Fri 8:30am–midnight; Sat 10am–midnight; Sun 10am–11pm. $2–$15.*

USS Midway at the Embarcadero.

3 Embarcadero. Take a leisurely stroll down San Diego's waterfront, where the sights include the flotilla of historic vessels that make up the San Diego Maritime Museum. Most impressive is the *Star of India,* which was originally put to sea in 1863, making it the world's oldest active ship. Continue to the Broadway Pier where you can catch the ferry to Coronado. ⏱ *30 min. Broadway Pier, 1050 N. Harbor Dr., at the intersection of Broadway.* ☎ *800/442-7847 or 619/234-4111. Ferries run Sun–Thurs on the hour 9am–9pm; Fri–Sat until 10pm. They return from the Ferry Landing in Coronado to the Broadway Pier Sun–Thurs every hour on the half-hour 9:30am–9:30pm; Fri–Sat until 10:30pm. The ride takes 15 min. The fare is $3.50 each way. Buy tickets at the Harbor Excursion* kiosk on Broadway Pier or at the Ferry Landing in Coronado. The ferries do not accommodate cars.

4 ★★★ Hotel del Coronado. This is the last of California's stately old seaside hotels. In continuous operation since 1888, the hotel is a monument to Victorian grandeur, boasting cupolas, turrets, and gingerbread trim, making it San Diego's most recognizable property. There is plenty here to engage a nonguest, including a gallery devoted to the hotel's history, a shopping arcade, and several wonderful options for drinks or dining—not to mention the fact that the hotel sits on one of San Diego's best beaches. ⏱ *1 hr. 1500 Orange Ave.* ☎ *800/468-3533 or 619/435-6611. www.hoteldel.com. Bus: 904 from the Ferry Landing.* ●

Balboa Park

1 Marston House
2 Cabrillo Bridge
3 San Diego Museum of Man
4 Old Globe Theatre
5 Alcazar Garden
6 Mingei International Museum
7 San Diego Museum of Art
8 Timken Museum of Art
9 Visitors Center
10 Palm Canyon
11 Japanese Friendship Garden Tea Pavilion
12 Spreckels Organ Pavilion
13 House of Pacific Relations International Cottages
14 San Diego Automotive Museum
15 San Diego Air & Space Museum
16 San Diego Hall of Champions Sports Museum
17 Botanical Building & Lily Pond
18 Museum of Photographic Arts
19 San Diego Model Railroad Museum
20 Reuben H. Fleet Science Center
21 San Diego Natural History Museum
22 Spanish Village Art Center
23 Balboa Park Miniature Railroad & Carousel
24 Gardens

Previous page: Mission Basilica San Diego de Alcalá.

Established in 1868, Balboa Park is the second-oldest city park in the United States. Much of its striking architecture, which now houses a variety of museums, was the product of the 1915–16 Panama–California Exposition and the 1935–36 California Pacific International Exposition. What makes Balboa Park unique is its extensive and mature botanical collection, owing largely to the efforts of Kate Sessions, a horticulturist who devoted her life to transforming the desolate mesas and scrub-filled canyons into the oases they are today (see p 9, bullet ❷). ***Note:*** The park encompasses 15 museums, so try to visit the two or three that most appeal to you. START: **Bus 1, 3, 7, or 120 to Balboa Park.**

❶ ★ **Marston House.** This elegant Craftsman home was built for a local businessman in 1905 by noted architects Irving Gill and William Hebbard. Listed on the National Register of Historic Places, the house features classic furnishings and art pottery, and is open for tours. ⏱ *45 min.* ☎ *619/297-9327 or 298-3142. www.sohosandiego. org. Admission $8 adults, $6 seniors, $4 children 6–12, free for kids 5 and under. Fri–Sun 10am–5pm.*

❷ ★ **Cabrillo Bridge.** Offering excellent views of downtown, the bridge straddles scenic, sycamore-lined Highway 163 and provides a dramatic entrance to the park. Built in 1915 for the Panama–California

The Old Globe Theatre.

Inside the Museum of Man.

Exposition, it's patterned after a bridge in Ronda, Spain. Directly ahead are the Museum of Man's distinctive California Tower and the park's main thoroughfare, El Prado. *This is the west-side entrance to the park; Laurel St. leads directly to the bridge.*

❸ ★ kids **San Diego Museum of Man.** This anthropological museum has an emphasis on the peoples of North and South America; there are also Egyptian mummies and relics, and a museum store with great folk art. The exterior doubled as part of Kane's mansion in the 1941 Orson Welles classic *Citizen Kane*; historical figures carved on the facade include conquistador Juan Rodríguez Cabrillo, Spanish Kings Charles I and Phillip III, and, at the very top, Father Junípero Serra. ⏱ *1 hr.* ☎ *619/239-2001. www.museum ofman.org. Admission $10 adults, $7.50 seniors, students, and active-duty military, $5 children 3–12, free for children 2 and under. Daily 10am–4:30pm.*

❹ ★★★ **Old Globe Theatre.** This is actually a three-theater complex that includes the Old Globe, an outdoor stage, and a small theater-in-the-round. Built for the 1935 exposition as a replica of Shakespeare's

The Mingei Museum.

original theater, the Globe was meant to be demolished after the fair but was saved by a group of dedicated citizens. In 1978, an arsonist destroyed the theater, which was rebuilt into what you see today; the facility also received a sweeping renovation for its 75th anniversary in 2010. ⏲ 10 min. ☎ 619/234-5623. www.theoldglobe.org. Backstage tours are offered most weekends at 10:30am and cost $5 for adults, $2 for students, seniors, and military. Performances are Tues–Sun, with weekend matinees. The box office is open Mon (and other nonperformance days) noon–6pm; Tues–Sun noon–8pm. Tickets $39–$85.

⑤ ★ Alcazar Garden. This formal garden is patterned after the ones surrounding the Alcazar Castle in Sevilla, Spain. The large tree at the rear is an Indian laurel fig, planted by Kate Sessions when the park was first landscaped. ⏲ 10 min. Free admission. Open 24 hr. but caution should be exercised after dark.

⑥ ★★ Mingei International Museum. The Mingei offers changing exhibitions that celebrate folk art, including textiles, costumes, jewelry, toys, pottery, paintings, and sculpture. The gift shop alone is worth a visit. ⏲ At least 30 min.

☎ 619/239-0003. www.mingei.org. Admission $7 adults, $5 seniors, $4 children 6–17 and students and military with ID, free for children 5 and under. Tues–Sun 10am–4pm.

⑦ ★ San Diego Museum of Art. The exquisite facade was inspired by the famous university building in Salamanca, Spain. The three life-size figures over the scalloped entryway are the Spanish painters Bartolomé Murillo, Francisco de Zurbarán, and Diego Velázquez. The museum holds San Diego's most extensive collection of fine art; major touring exhibitions are presented, as well. There's also an ongoing schedule of concerts, films, and lectures, usually themed with a current show. ⏲ At least 1 hr. ☎ 619/232-7931. www.sdmart. org. Admission $12 adults, $9 seniors and military, $8 students, $4.50 children 6–17, free for children 5 and under. Admission to traveling exhibits varies; the Sculpture Garden is always free. Tues–Sat 10am–5pm; Sun noon–5pm.

The San Diego Museum of Art.

8 ★ Timken Museum of Art. This small, always-free museum houses a collection of 19th-century American paintings and works by European old masters, as well as a worthy display of Russian icons and San Diego's only Rembrandt painting. ⏱ *30 min.* ☎ *619/239-5548. www.timkenmuseum.org. Free admission. Tues–Sat 10am–4:30pm; Sun 1:30–4:30pm.*

9 Visitors Center. Pick up maps, souvenirs, and discount tickets to the museums; guided and self-guided tours begin here, too. In the courtyard behind the Visitors Center, you'll find the beautiful *Woman of Tehuantepec* fountain sculpture by Donal Hord, as well as the Prado restaurant, see p 10, bullet **3**.

10 ★ Palm Canyon. Fifty species of palm, plus magnolia trees and a Moreton Bay fig tree, provide a tropical canopy along this short, dead-end walkway. It's secluded, so it's not recommended you venture here after dark. ⏱ *15 min. Free admission. Open 24 hr.*

The tranquil **11 ★ Tea Pavilion** at the **Japanese Friendship Garden** serves fresh sushi, noodle soups, and Asian salads—it also carries quirky imported Japanese candies and beverages in addition to some familiar American snacks. The teahouse overlooks an 11½-acre (5-hectare) canyon that has been carefully developed to include traditional Japanese elements, including a small meditation garden. ☎ *619/231-0048. www.cohnrestaurants. com. Tea Pavilion admission is free; admission to the garden is $4 adults, $2.50 seniors, students, and military, free for children under 7. Tues–Sun 10am–4pm; Mon–Fri 10am–5pm; Sat–Sun 10am–4pm in summer.*

Portrait of Marguerite de Sève, the Timken Museum of Art.

☎ *619/232-2721 for information about the museum, or visit www. niwa.org.*

12 ★ Spreckels Organ Pavilion. Famed contralto Ernestine Schumann-Heink sang at the December 31, 1914, dedication of the Spreckles Organ Pavilion, donated to San Diego by brothers John D. and

Palm Canyon.

The Spreckels Organ Museum.

Adolph B. Spreckels. Free recitals are performed on one of the largest outdoor organs in the world (its vast structure contains 4,530 pipes) on Sundays at 2pm, with additional concerts and events scheduled in summertime. ⏱ *15 min.* ☎ *619/702-8138. www.sosorgan.com. Free admission.*

🔞 **House of Pacific Relations International Cottages.** This cluster of 17 cottages disseminates information about the culture, traditions, and history of more than 30 countries. Special events are presented by one of the nations every Sunday, 2 to 3pm, March through October. ⏱ *At least 15 min.* ☎ *619/234-0739. www. sdhpr.org. Free admission. Sun noon–4pm; 4th Tues of each month 11am–3pm. The adjacent United Nations*

Building houses an international gift shop where you can buy jewelry, toys, books, and UNICEF greeting cards. ☎ *619/233-5044. Daily 10am–4:30pm.*

🔞 ★ **San Diego Automotive Museum.** Whether you're a gearhead into muscle cars or someone who appreciates the sculptural beauty of fine design, this museum has something for you. It features a changing roster of exhibits, as well as a permanent collection of fabulous wheels. ⏱ *At least 30 min.* ☎ *619/231-2886. www.sdauto museum.org. Admission $8 adults, $6 seniors and active military, $5 students, $4 children 6–15, free for children 5 and under. Daily 10am–5pm (last admission 4:30pm).*

The Air & Space Museum.

15 ★★ **kids** **San Diego Air & Space Museum.** This kid-pleaser has more than 60 aircraft on display, providing an overview of aeronautical history, from the days of hot-air balloons to the space age. ⏱ *1 hr.* ☎ *619/234-8291. www.sandiegoairandspace.org. Admission $15 adults, $12 seniors and students, $6 children 3–11, free for active military with ID and children 2 and under. Sept–May daily 10am–4:30pm; June–Aug daily 10am–5:30pm.*

16 **San Diego Hall of Champions Sports Museum.** From baseball great Ted Williams to Olympic gold medalist Shaun White, San Diego's best-ever athletes and the sports they played are celebrated by this slick museum. You can try out your play-by-play skills at the more than 25 exhibits, rotating art shows, and interactive stations. ⏱ *1 hr.* ☎ *619/234-2544. www. sdhoc.com. Admission $8 adults, $6 seniors, students, and military, $4 children 7–17, free for children 6 and under. Daily 10am–4:30pm.*

17 ★ **Botanical Building and Lily Pond.** This serene park within the park is a great retreat on a hot day; ferns, orchids, impatiens, begonias, and other plants—about 2,100 tropical and flowering varieties, plus rotating exhibits—are sheltered here. The graceful 250-foot-long (76m) building, part of the 1915 Panama–California Exposition, is one of the world's largest wood-lath structures. The lily pond out front attracts sun worshippers, painters, and buskers. ⏱ *15 min.* ☎ *619/235-1100. Free admission. Fri–Wed 10am–4pm; closed Thurs and major holidays.*

18 ★★ **Museum of Photographic Arts.** This is one of the few museums in the United States devoted exclusively to the

The Lily Pond at the Botanical Building.

photographic arts, encompassing not only traditional photography, but also cinema, video, and digital art. There's also a plush cinema that screens classic films on an ongoing basis and a great bookstore. ⏱ *At least 30 min.* ☎ *619/238-7559. www.mopa.org. Admission $6 adults, $4 seniors, students, and military, free for children under 12 with adult. Tues–Sun 10am–5pm.*

19 ★ **kids** **San Diego Model Railroad Museum.** Kids and train buffs will love the scale-model railroads depicting Southern California's transportation history and terrain with an astounding attention to miniature details. ⏱ *30 min. Located in the Casa de Balboa,*

Botanical Building, Balboa Park.

Passport to Balboa Park

If you plan to visit more than three of the park's museums, buy the Passport to Balboa Park—it allows entrance to 14 museums and attractions, and is valid for 1 week. It's $45 for adults, $24 for children 3 to 12. If you plan to spend a day at the zoo and return for the museums another day, buy the Zoo/Passport combo ($75 adults, $39 children). The Stay-for-the-Day pass gives you 1-day access to five museums for $35 (adults only). The passports can be purchased at any participating attraction (except the zoo), at the visitor center, or online at www.balboapark.org.

below the Museum of Photographic Arts. ☎ 619/696-0199. www.sdmrm. org. Admission $7 adults, $6 seniors, $3 students, $2.50 military; free for children under 15. Tues–Fri 11am–4pm; Sat–Sun 11am–5pm.

20 ★★ kids **Reuben H. Fleet Science Center.** A must-see for kids of any age, this tantalizing collection of interactive exhibits and virtual rides is designed to stimulate the imagination and teach scientific principles. There is also an IMAX

The Museum of Natural History.

dome theater, which is used for planetarium shows the first Wednesday of each month at 7 and 8pm. ⏱ At least 1 hr. ☎ 619/238-1233. www.rhfleet.org. Fleet Experience admission includes an IMAX film and exhibit galleries: $15 adults, $12 seniors and children 3–12 (exhibit gallery can be purchased individually, $10 adults, $9 seniors and children); planetarium show: $11 adults, $9 seniors and kids 3–12. Hours vary but always daily 9:30am–5pm; later closing times possible.

21 kids **San Diego Natural History Museum.** Founded in 1874, this is one of the West's oldest scientific institutions, focusing on the flora, fauna, and mineralogy of the region. The museum shows 3-D nature films in its giant-screen theater, and also presents special exhibitions, leads free nature hikes, and has a full schedule of classes, lectures, and overnight expeditions for both families and adults. ⏱ At least 1 hr. ☎ 619/232-3821. www.sdnhm. org. Admission $16 adults, $14 seniors, $11 students, kids age 13–17, and active-duty military, $10 children 3–12, free for children 2 and under. Two films in the museum's theater are included with admission. Daily 10am–5pm.

22 ★ **Spanish Village Art Center.** This collection of 37 picture-perfect *casitas* is home to more than 250 artists, specializing in everything from glass blowing to woodcarving. Many of the artists work on-site, allowing you to watch the art-making process. ⏱ *20 min.* ☎ *619/233-9050. www.spanish villageart.com. Free admission. Daily 11am–4pm.*

23 kids **Balboa Park Miniature Railroad and Carousel.** The open-air railroad takes a 3-minute journey through a grove of eucalyptus trees, while the carousel, built in 1910, is one of the last to still offer a ring grab. ⏱ *20 min. Zoo Dr., next to San Diego Zoo entrance. Railroad* ☎ *619/231-1515. www.sandiego zoo.org. Summer daily 11am–6:30pm; Sept–May weekends and holidays only 11am–4:30pm. Carousel* ☎ *619/239-0512. www.balboa park.org. Summer daily 11am–5pm; Sept–May weekends and holidays only 11am–5pm. Admission $2 Railroad (free for children under 1), $2 Carousel.*

The Spanish Village Art Center.

24 ★★ **Gardens.** Cross Park Boulevard via a pedestrian overpass and you'll find, to your left, a Desert Garden, and to your right, the Inez Grant Parker Memorial Rose Garden, home to some 2,500 roses. (Blooms peak Mar–May.) ⏱ *20 min. www. balboapark.org. Free admission. Open 24 hr. but not recommended after dark.*

Balboa Park's Desert Garden.

San Diego **with Kids**

1 San Diego Zoo
2 Corvette Diner
3 SeaWorld San Diego
4 San Diego Zoo Safari Park
5 LEGOLAND California
6 Reuben H. Fleet Science Center
7 Birch Aquarium at Scripps
8 Whale watching
9 San Diego Model Railroad Museum
10 Chula Vista Nature Center
11 The New Children's Museum
12 Belmont Park

In San Diego, activities abound for kids—from toddlers to teens. With its renowned theme parks and zoo, and its kid-friendly museums (where unsuspecting young minds just might learn a thing or two), San Diego more than lives up to its reputation as a family vacation destination. Best of all, these places won't bore the adults in tow either. START: **Bus 7 to the San Diego Zoo in Balboa Park.**

1 ★★★ **San Diego Zoo.** San Diego's world-famous zoo appeals to children of all ages, and the double-decker bus tours bring all the animals into easy view of even the smallest visitors. There's a Children's Zoo where kids can feed and pet the animals, as well as a popular show featuring trained sea lions *See p 17, bullet* **1**.

Get a taste of the rockin' 1950s at the **2** **Corvette Diner,** where the jukebox is loud and the gum-snapping waitresses slide into your booth to take your order. The restaurant has several themed rooms and an arcade with everything from air hockey to Guitar Hero. *2965 Historic Decatur Rd. (in Liberty Station, off Rosecrans St.).* ☎ *619/542-1476. www.cohnrestaurants.com. $9–$15 (kids' plates $7).*

3 ★★ **SeaWorld San Diego.** Crowd-pleasing shows and rides highlight this marine-life theme

Meerkats at the San Diego Zoo.

park, made politically correct with a nominally informative atmosphere. The 20-minute shows—starring orcas, dolphins, sea lions, household pets, and (in summer) human acrobats—run several times throughout the day. Several successive 4-ton (3,629kg) killer whales have functioned as the park's mascot, Shamu, who performs in a

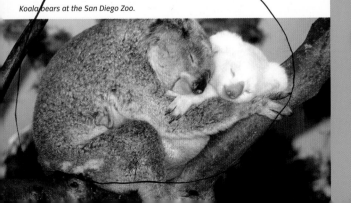

Koala bears at the San Diego Zoo.

Dolphins at SeaWorld.

7-million-gallon pool with see-through walls. SeaWorld's real strength, though, are the simulated marine environments, including Wild Arctic (with beluga whales, walruses, and polar bears), Manatee Rescue, the Shark Encounter, and—everyone's favorite—the Penguin Encounter. ⏱ *At least 3 hr. 500 SeaWorld Dr.* ☎ *800/257-4268 or 619/226-3901. www.seaworld.com. Admission $69 adults, $59 children 3–9, free for children 2 and under. Hours vary seasonally, but always at least daily 10am–5pm; most weekends and during summer 9am–11pm. Parking $12. Bus: 8/9.*

➍ ★★★ **San Diego Zoo Safari Park.** Originally a breeding facility for the San Diego Zoo, the 1,800-acre (728-hectare) Safari Park now holds 3,500 animals representing some 430 different species. Many of the animals roam freely in vast enclosures, allowing giraffes to interact with antelopes, much as they would in Africa. Although the San Diego Zoo may be "world famous," it's the Safari Park that many visitors celebrate as their favorite. Roar & Snore sleepovers, which are held year-round (except Dec–Jan) on most Fridays and Saturdays—with extended dates in summer—let you camp out next to the animal compound (reservations required). ⏱ *At least 3 hr. 15500 San Pasqual Valley Rd.* ☎ *760/747-8702. www.sandiego zoo.ord/park. Admission $37 adults, $27 children 3–11, free for children 2 and under and active-duty military (U.S. and foreign). Daily 9am–4pm (grounds close at 5pm); extended hours during summer and Festival of Lights (2 weekends in Dec). Parking $9. Bus: 386 (Mon–Sat). The park is 34 miles (55km) north of downtown San Diego in a rural setting, making a car almost a necessity.*

A giraffe at the San Diego Zoo Safari Park.

Admission Discounts

San Diego's three main animal attractions offer combo tickets that can save you some cash. If you plan to visit both the zoo and Safari Park, a 2-Visit Pass is $70 for adults, $50 for children 3 to 11; passes are valid for 1 year and can be used twice at the same attraction if you choose. A 3-for-1 pass gives you 1-day passes to the zoo and Safari Park, plus unlimited entry to SeaWorld for 5 days from first use; the cost is $121 adults, $99 children ages 3 to 9.

Other value options include the **Southern California CityPass** (☎ 888/330-5008; www.citypass.com), which covers the zoo or Safari Park, as well as SeaWorld, Disneyland Resorts, and Universal Studios in Los Angeles. Passes are $269 for adults, and $229 for kids age 3 to 9 (a savings of about 30%), valid for 14 days. The **Go San Diego Card** (☎ 866/628-9032; www.gosandiegocard.com) offers unlimited general admission to more than 50 attractions, including the zoo and LEGOLAND, as well as deals on shopping, dining, and day trips to Mexico. One-day packages start at $69 for adults and $58 for children (ages 3–12).

---

5 ★ **LEGOLAND California.**
This theme park in Carlsbad, 40 minutes north of downtown San Diego, offers a full day of entertainment for families. There are more than 50 rides, shows, and attractions, including hands-on interactive displays; scale models of international landmarks (the Eiffel Tower, for example) constructed of LEGO bricks; and a water park with slides and pools. LEGOLAND is geared toward children ages 2 to 12, with just enough of a thrill-ride component that preteens will be amused; but most teenagers will find this place a bit of a snooze. A sister attraction, Sea Life Aquarium, is next door, displaying live fish in giant tanks. ⏲ *At least 3 hr. 1 Legoland Dr.* ☎ *877/ 534-6526 or 760/918-5346. www. legoland.com or www.sealifeus.com. LEGOLAND $67 adults, $57 seniors and children 3–12, free to children 2 and under; water park additional $10 per person. Sea Life $19 adults, $16 seniors, $12 children; discounted 1- or*

2-day park-hopper tickets available. July–Aug daily 10am–8pm; June daily 10am–5 or 6pm; off season Thurs– Mon 10am–5 or 6pm. Closed Tues– Wed Sept–May, but open daily during winter and spring vacation periods. Parking $12. Bus: 321. From San Diego, you'll need a car.

6 ★★ **Reuben H. Fleet Science Center.** With its hands-on exhibits, motion simulator rides, and an IMAX theater, this science fun house draws kids like magnets. *See p 26, bullet* **20**.

7 ★★ **Birch Aquarium at Scripps.** This beautiful facility is both an aquarium and a museum, operated as the interpretive arm of the world-famous Scripps Institution of Oceanography. The aquarium affords close-up views of marine life from the Pacific Northwest and California coasts, Mexico's Sea of Cortés, and the tropical seas, all presented in more than 60 tanks; the giant kelp forest is particularly

The Birch Aquarium at Scripps.

impressive. The outdoor demonstration tide pool also offers amazing coastal views. ⏱ *90 min. 2300 Expedition Way.* ☎ *858/534-3474. www. aquarium.ucsd.edu. Admission $12 adults, $9 seniors and college students, $8.50 children 3–17, free for children 2 and under. Daily 9am–5pm. Free parking. Bus: 30.*

⑧ ★★ Whale-Watching. The easiest (and cheapest) way to observe the migration of the Pacific gray whales every mid-December to mid-March is to head to Cabrillo National Monument (see p 13, bullet ❶), where you'll find a glassed-in observatory and educational whale exhibits. Better yet, head to sea—the variety of options includes sailboats, large ships with lots of amenities, and kayak tours. *Whakapono Sailing Charters, based in Mission Bay (☎ 800/659-0141 or 619/988-9644; www.whakapono.us), offers two trips per day (8:30am and 1pm); each lasts 3 hr. and carries a maximum of 6 passengers. $75 per person (minimum 2 passengers), including beverages and snacks. OEX Dive & Kayak Centers (☎ 858/454-6195; www.oexcalifornia.com) leads guided kayak tours in search of*

passing whales. It's about a 1-mile (1.6km) paddle that departs daily at 1pm from La Jolla Shores. Cost is $65. Embarcadero-based companies that offer engine-driven expeditions include Hornblower Cruises (☎ 888/467-6256 or 619/686-8715; www. hornblower.com) and San Diego Harbor Excursion (☎ 800/442-7847 or 619/234-4111; www.sdhe.com). Trips are 3 or 3½ hr., and fares run $30–$37 for adults, with discounts for seniors, military, and kids.

⑨ ★ San Diego Model Railroad Museum. This 27,000-square-foot (2,508 sq. m) space has four permanent scale-model railroad dioramas, along with interactive multimedia displays, to fire the imagination of train lovers of all ages. *See p 25, bullet ⑲.*

⑩ ★★ Chula Vista Nature Center. Overshadowed by Sea-World and the zoo, this wonderful, interactive nature center is about 15 minutes south of downtown. It highlights the plants and animals native to San Diego Bay and the surrounding wetlands, featuring exhibits of sea turtles, stingrays, and small sharks in kid-level open tanks.

🕐 At least 1 hr. 1000 Gunpowder Point Dr. ☎ 619/409-5900. www.chulavistanaturecenter.org. $11 adults, $8 seniors, students, and kids ages 12–17, $6 children 4–11, free for children 3 and under. Tues–Sun 10am–5pm. The (free) parking lot is located away from the center, and a shuttle bus ferries guests btw. the two points every 10–15 min. (last shuttle at 4pm). Trolley: Blue Line to Bayfront/E St. (request shuttle at trolley info center).

⓫ ★ **The New Children's Museum.** This $25-million, state-of-the-art facility opened in 2008, and features local artists' ever-changing pieces that can be climbed on, touched, or interacted with (they just might intrigue the adults in tow, as well). The downtown space also offers lots of arts-based classes and good old-fashioned play areas; it will appeal mostly to the under-13 set. 🕐 1 hr. 200 W. Island Ave. (at Front St.). ☎ 619/233-8792. www.thinkplaycreate.org. Admission $10, $5 seniors and military, free for children under 1; free admission the 2nd Sun of the month. Mon–Tues and Fri–Sat 10am–4pm; Thurs

10am–6pm; Sun noon–4pm (2nd Sun of the month 10am–4pm). Parking $10. Bus: 3, 11, 120, or 992. Trolley: Orange Line to Convention Center.

⓬ **Belmont Park.** This seaside amusement park in Mission Beach first opened in 1925 as a means to lure people to the then-scarcely pop-ulated coastal areas. There are plenty of carnival-style rides, but the star attractions are the Giant Dipper roller coaster and the Plunge, a huge indoor pool. Both are Roaring '20s originals. Recent years have seen the addition of the Wave House, which features unique wave machines that produce rides for both novice and advanced surfers and bodyboarders. It's a blast to watch the pros in action. 🕐 2 hr. 3190 Mission Blvd. (at W. Mission Bay Dr.). ☎ 858/488-1549. www.giantdipper.com. Rides are $2–$6 each; unlimited-ride wrist-bands are $23 (for those over 50 inches/127cm) and $16 (under 50 inches/127cm); wave rides start at $20 per hr., with a one-time registra-tion fee of $10. Daily 11am–8pm (weekend and summer hours later; closed Mon–Thurs Jan–Feb). Bus: 8/9.

The Giant Dipper at Belmont Park.

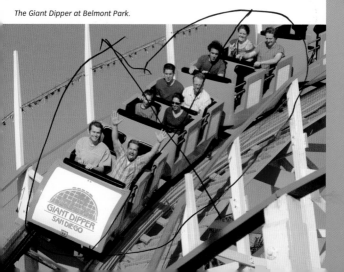

Historic San Diego

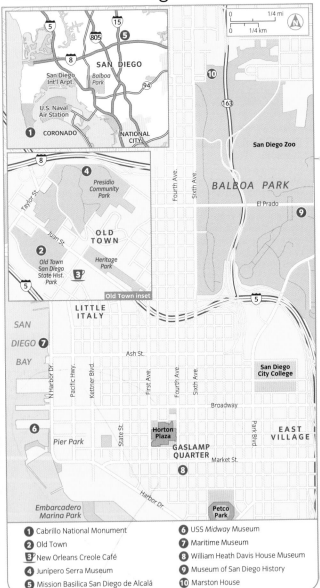

1. Cabrillo National Monument
2. Old Town
3. New Orleans Creole Café
4. Junípero Serra Museum
5. Mission Basilica San Diego de Alcalá
6. USS *Midway* Museum
7. Maritime Museum
8. William Heath Davis House Museum
9. Museum of San Diego History
10. Marston House

S an Diego is where California began. Conquistador Juan Rodríguez Cabrillo first claimed the region in the name of Spain in 1542, but it would be more than 220 years before they sent an occupying force to colonize Alta California. In 1769, soldiers and missionaries, including Father Junipero Serra, set up camp on Presidio Hill overlooking what is now Old Town, making it the first European settlement in California. San Diego would eventually grow into a Wild West boomtown, complete with characters such as famed lawman Wyatt Earp. And even from the earliest days of the 20th century, the United States military coveted San Diego's strategic geographic location, making it the bastion of military heritage it remains today. If you like to bolster your trips with a little history, San Diego is an excellent choice with lots to offer. START: **Bus 84.**

① ★★★ kids **Cabrillo National Monument.** From the park's location high atop Point Loma, you can overlook San Diego Bay and see the spot where Juan Cabrillo came ashore and met with some very concerned Kumeyaay Indians in 1542. There are also museum installations describing the point's long military history; the cemetery you pass on the way into the park is Fort Rosecrans National Cemetery, a military graveyard since the 1870s. *See p 13, bullet* ①.

② ★ **Old Town.** The flags of Spain, Mexico, and the United States flew in succession over the dusty pueblo of San Diego, a rough-and-tumble outpost of frontier settlers. History comes alive daily in Old Town State Historic Park (see p 9, bullet ①), where you can wander the original town square, lined with reconstructed and original buildings re-creating the era from 1821–72. The structures now serve as museums, shops, and restaurants. Directly south of the park, along San Diego Avenue, are more curio stores and dining options, as well as the Whaley House museum, which attracts attention far and wide for its reputation of being certifiably haunted. A little farther down the street is El Campo

Santo, the town's original cemetery. A block east of the Whaley House is Heritage Park, a collection of seven gorgeously restored Victorian buildings, including Southern California's first synagogue. *Whaley House:* 🕐 *30 min. 2476 San Diego Ave.* ☎ *619/297-7511. www.whaley house.org. Admission before 5pm $6 adults, $5 seniors over 54, $4 children 3–12; admission after 5pm $10 adults, $5 children 3–12. Free for children 2 and under. May–Sept daily 10am–9:30pm; Oct–Apr Sun–Tues*

The Cabrillo National Monument.

Historic Old Town.

10am–5pm, Thurs–Sat 10am–9:30pm. Heritage Park: ⏱ 20 min. 2450 Heritage Park Row (corner of Juan and Harney sts.). ☎ 619/819-6009. www.heritageparksd.com. Free admission. Daily sunrise to sunset. Trolley: Blue or Green Line to Old Town.

Junipero Serra Museum.

When you're seated on the lovely patio of the small ⑤P **New Orleans Creole Café,** amid the shade trees of the Whaley House complex, you won't mind a little geographical incongruity one bit. You'll happily enjoy your po' boy, gumbo, or muffuletta while the throngs line up elsewhere for mediocre Mexican food. *2476 A San Diego Ave. (behind the Whaley House gift shop).* ☎ *619/542-1698. www.new orleanscreolecafe.com. $11–$20.*

④ ★ **Junipero Serra Museum.** Perched on a hill above Old Town, this Spanish Mission–style structure is located where, in 1769, the first mission, first presidio, and first non-native settlement on the west coast of the United States were founded. This is the "Plymouth Rock of the Pacific Coast." The museum's exhibits introduce visitors to the Native American, Spanish, and Mexican people who first called this place home; on display are their belongings, from cannons to cookware. Built in 1929, the stately building offers great views from its 70-foot (21m) tower. Presidio Park, which was established around the museum, is a nice place for a picnic, and has surprisingly extensive walking trails. ⏱ 1 hr. 2727 Presidio Dr. ☎ 619/232-6203. www.sandiego history.org. Admission $5 adults; $4 seniors, students, and military; $2 children 6–17; free for children 5 and under. Sat–Sun 10am–5pm. Trolley: Blue or Green Line to Old Town.

⑤ **Mission Basilica San Diego de Alcalá.** This was the first link in a chain of 21 missions founded by Spanish missionary Junipero Serra. In 1774, the mission was moved from Old Town to its present site for agricultural reasons and to separate the indigenous converts from the

Mission Basilica San Diego de Alcalá.

fortress that included the original building. The mission was sacked by the local tribe a year after it was built, leading Father Serra to reconstruct it using 5- to 7-foot-thick (1.5m–2.1m) adobe walls and clay tile roofs, rendering it harder to burn. In the process, he inspired a bevy of 20th-century California architects. Mass is said daily in this active Catholic parish. ***Note:*** In the North County city of Oceanside you can also visit **Mission San Luis Rey de Francia,** 4050 Mission Ave. (☎ 760/757-3651; www.sanluisrey. org). Known as the "King of the Missions," it's California's largest, founded in 1798. ⏱ *30 min.* **10818**

Spooks & Splashes

Those who want to take a walk on the supernatural side can stroll through Old Town with **"ghost hunter" Michael Brown** (☎ 619/972-3900; www.oldtownsmosthaunted.com). He leads tours in search of real paranormal activity Thursday through Sunday at 9 and 11pm; tickets are $19 adults, $10 children 6 to 12, and free for kids 5 and under. **Haunted San Diego Tours** (☎ 877/642-8683 or 619/255-6170; www.hauntedsandiegotours.com) features costumed storytellers spinning supernatural yarns aboard the "ghost bus" as you visit some of the city's most mysterious sites. Tours run Thursday through Monday at 7pm, with an additional 9pm trip in summer. Tickets are $35 (it's not recommended for children under 10).

The 90-minute amphibious **SEAL (Sea and Land Adventures) tour** (☎ 619/298-8687; or visit www.historictours.com) departs from Seaport Village and motors along the Embarcadero before splashing into San Diego Bay. The narrated tour gives you the maritime and military history of San Diego from the right perspective. Trips are scheduled daily, April through October, 10am to 5pm (Thurs through Mon, 10am to 4pm, Nov to Mar). The cost is $32 for adults and $16 for kids 4 to 12 (free for children 3 and under).

The USS Midway *Museum.*

San Diego Mission Rd. ☎ 619/281-8449. www.missionsandiego.com. Admission $3 adults, $2 seniors and students, $1 children under 12. Free Sun and for daily Masses. Daily 9am–4:45pm; Mass daily 7am and 5:30pm, and Sun at 8, 10, 11am, and noon. Trolley: Green Line to Mission San Diego.

⑥ **USS *Midway* Museum.** The USS *Midway* had a 47-year military history that began 1 week after the Japanese surrender of World War II in 1945. The carrier is now moored

Unconditional Surrender statue, near USS Midway *Museum.*

at the Embarcadero and has become the world's largest floating naval-aviation museum. A self-guided audio tour takes visitors to several levels of the ship, telling the story of life on board. The highlight is climbing up the superstructure to the bridge and gazing down on the 1,001-foot-long (305m) flight deck, with various aircraft poised for duty. **Note:** Be prepared to climb some stairs and ladders. ⏱ *1 hr. 910 Harbor Dr. (at Navy Pier).* ☎ *619/544-9600. www.midway.org. Admission $18 adults; $15 seniors and students; $10 retired military and children 6–17, free for children 5 and under and active-duty military. Daily 10am–5pm. Bus: 2, 210, or 992. Trolley: Orange or Blue Line to America Plaza.*

⑦ ★★ **kids Maritime Museum.** This flotilla of classic ships is led by the full-rigged merchant vessel *Star of India* (1863), a National Historic Landmark and the world's oldest ship that still goes to sea. The collection also includes the HMS *Surprise*, a painstakingly accurate reproduction of an 18th-century Royal Navy Frigate, which played a supporting role to Russell Crowe in the film *Master and Commander*, and a 300-foot-long (91m) Cold War–era B-39 Soviet attack submarine. You can board and tour each vessel. ⏱ *90 min. 1492 N.*

Harbor Dr. ☎ *619/234-9153. www. sdmaritime.org. Admission $14 adults; $11 seniors over 62 and active-duty military; $8 children 6–17; free for children 5 and under. Daily 9am–8pm (till 9pm in summer). Bus: Numerous routes including 2, 923, or 992. Trolley: Blue Line to County Center/Little Italy.*

8 William Heath Davis House Museum. Shipped by boat to San Diego in 1850 from Portland, Maine, this is the oldest structure in the Gaslamp Quarter. It is a well-preserved example of a prefabricated "saltbox" family home and has remained structurally unchanged for more than 150 years, though it originally stood at another location. A museum on the first and second floors documents life in "New Town," and profiles some of the city's early movers and shakers. The Gaslamp Quarter Historical Foundation also makes its home here, and it has a nice gift store in the basement. ⏱ *30 min. 410 Island Ave. (at Fourth Ave.).* ☎ *619/233-4692. www.gaslamp quarter.org. Admission $5; $4 seniors, military, and students. Tues–Sat 10am–6pm; Sun 9am–3pm. The Historical Foundation offers walking tours of the neighborhood for $10 ($8 for seniors, students, and military), Sat at 11am. Bus: 3, 11, or 120.*

Inside the Davis House.

Trolley: Gaslamp Quarter or Convention Center.

9 Museum of San Diego History. Operated by the San Diego Historical Society, this Balboa Park museum offers permanent and changing exhibits on topics related to the history of the region. Many of the museum's photographs depict Balboa Park and the growth of the city. Books and other items relating to San Diego history are available in the gift shop, and the research library downstairs is open Wednesday through Saturday (9:30am– 1pm). ⏱ *45 min. 1649 El Prado, in Casa del Balboa.* ☎ *619/232-6203. www.sandiegohistory.org. Admission $5 adults, $4 seniors, students, and military, $2 children 6–17, free for children 5 and under. Tues–Sun 10am–5pm. Bus: 7.*

10 ★ Marston House. Noted San Diego architects Irving Gill and William Hebbard designed this Craftsman house in 1905 for George Marston, a local businessman and philanthropist. Listed on the National Register of Historic Places, the home's interior is furnished with decor from the Arts and Crafts period, including Roycroft, Stickley, and Limbert pieces, as well as art pottery. *See p 64. Bus: 3 or 120.*

The Best **Golf Courses**

Balboa Park Municipal
Golf Course 4
Coronado Municipal
Golf Course 5
Park Hyatt Aviara Golf
Club 1
Riverwalk Golf Club 3
Torrey Pines Golf Course 2

With its mild year-round climate and nearly 100 courses, half of them public, San Diego County is an ideal destination for golfers. This selection includes acclaimed courses for hard-core aficionados and easily accessed greens for casual duffers. All take advantage of San Diego's diverse terrain, from canyons and mesas to estuaries and ocean. For a full list of San Diego courses, check out the San Diego Golf Pages (www.golfsd.com). San Diego Golf Reservations (☎ 866/717-6552 or 858/456-8300; www.sandiegogolf.com) can arrange tee times for you at the premier courses. START: **Bus 2.**

Balboa Park Municipal Golf Course.

Surrounded by the beauty of Balboa Park, this 18-hole course features fairways sprinkled with eucalyptus leaves and distractingly nice views of the San Diego skyline. It's convenient and affordable—the perfect choice for visitors who want to work some golf into their vacation, rather than the other way around. The course even rents clubs. *2600 Golf Course Dr. (off Pershing Dr. or 26th St. in the southeast corner of the park).* ☎ *619/570-1234 (automated reservation system) or 619/239-1660 (pro shop). www.sandiego.gov/golf. Nonresident fees $38 weekdays, $48 weekends; twilight rate $23 weekdays, $29 weekends; cart rental $28. Reservations are suggested at least a week in advance; first-come, first-served tee times offered from 6:30–7am. Bus: 2, exit at C and 26th sts., head north into the park.*

Coronado Municipal Golf Course.

The postcard vistas will test your powers of concentration at this 18-hole, par-72 course overlooking Glorietta Bay, the Coronado Bridge, and the downtown San Diego skyline. There's also a coffee shop, pro shop, and driving range on-site. Half of the daily tee times are awarded via a day-of-play lottery (6–8:59am); the rest can be obtained by calling ☎ 619/435-3122 up to 2 days out, or ☎ 619/435-3121 ext. 1, 3 to 14 days prior ($30 fee). If you don't win the lottery, you can still add your name to a standby list and step in for no-shows. *2000 Visalia Row.* ☎ *619/435-3121. www.golfcoronado.com. Greens fees $30; cart fees are $16 per person. Greens fees for twilight play are $15; cart rates are $11 per person. Club rental $50 ($30 twilight rate). Bus: 901, exit at Pomona Ave. and Glorietta Pl.*

The Park Hyatt Aviara Golf Club.

★★ Park Hyatt Aviara Golf Club.

In Carlsbad (40 min. north of downtown San Diego), Aviara was designed by Arnold Palmer and is uniquely landscaped to incorporate natural elements that blend in neatly with the protected Batiquitos Lagoon nearby. The course is 7,007 yards (6,407m) from the championship tees, laid out over rolling hillsides with plenty of bunker and water challenges (casual golfers may be frustrated). Practice areas are available for putting, chipping, sand play, and driving, and the pro shop and clubhouse are fully equipped. *7447 Batiquitos Dr.* ☎ *760/603-6900. www.parkaviara. hyatt.com. Greens fees Mon–Thurs $215 (including mandatory cart); Fri–Sun $235; afternoon rates start at 1:30pm in winter, 3pm in summer ($140 weekday, $145 weekend). Coaster: Carlsbad Village Station; cab it from there.*

★ Riverwalk Golf Club.

Redesigned by Ted Robinson and Ted Robinson, Jr., these links wandering along the Mission Valley floor are the most convenient courses for anyone staying downtown or near the beaches. Riverwalk sports a slick, upscale clubhouse; four lakes with waterfalls (in play on 13 of the 27 holes); open, undulating fairways; and trolley tracks on which a bright red trolley speeds through now and then without proving too distracting. *1150 Fashion Valley Rd.* ☎ *619/296-4563. www.riverwalkgc.com. Nonresident greens fees, including cart, $99 Mon–Thurs, $125 Fri–Sun; senior, twilight, and bargain evening rates are available. Trolley: Green Line to Fashion Valley Transit Center.*

★★★ Torrey Pines Golf Course.

These two gorgeous, municipal 18-hole championship courses, on the coast between La Jolla and Del Mar, are only 20 minutes from downtown San Diego. Home of the Farmers Insurance Open (formerly the Buick Invitational), and the setting for a memorable U.S. Open in 2008, Torrey Pines is second only to Pebble Beach as California's top golf destination. On a bluff overlooking the ocean, the north course is picturesque and has the signature hole (no. 6), but the south course is more challenging, has more sea-facing play, and benefits from a $3.5-million overhaul in 2002. *11480 Torrey Pines Rd.* ☎ *877/581-7171 (option 3 for automated reservations 8–90 days in advance; $41 booking fee) or 800/985-4653 for the pro shop and lessons. www.torreypinesgolfcourse. com or www.sandiego.gov/torrey pines. Greens fees on the south course $174 weekdays, $218 weekends; on the north course $95 weekdays, $119 weekends; twilight and senior rates available. Cart rentals $40. First-come, first-served tee times are available from sunup to 7:30am. Single golfers also stand a good chance of getting on the course if they just turn up and get on the waiting list for a threesome. Lessons assure you a spot on the course, and the pro shop rents clubs. Bus: 101.* ●

The Torrey Pines Golf Course.

Gaslamp Quarter

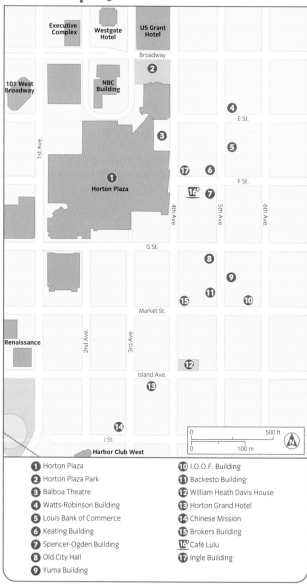

1. Horton Plaza
2. Horton Plaza Park
3. Balboa Theatre
4. Watts-Robinson Building
5. Louis Bank of Commerce
6. Keating Building
7. Spencer-Ogden Building
8. Old City Hall
9. Yuma Building
10. I.O.O.F. Building
11. Backesto Building
12. William Heath Davis House
13. Horton Grand Hotel
14. Chinese Mission
15. Brokers Building
16. Café Lulu
17. Ingle Building

Previous page: A house in Hillcrest.

A National Historic District covering some 16 city blocks, the Gaslamp Quarter features many Victorian-style commercial buildings built between the Civil War and World War I. The father of modern San Diego, Alonzo Horton, purchased 1,000 acres (405 hectares) of muddy, bayfront land for $260 in 1867 and ignited a real-estate boom. Horton's "New Town" is today's Gaslamp Quarter, featuring a proliferation of restaurants, shops, clubs, and hotels that make it a mirror image of its 1880s heyday. The Gaslamp Quarter is bound by Fourth Avenue to the west, Sixth Avenue to the east, Broadway to the north, and L Street and the waterfront to the south. It's all very walkable thanks to Horton's business savvy—he wanted to maximize his land sales, so he laid out small blocks (creating more desirable corner lots) with no alleys. START: **Any downtown bus to Horton Plaza, Blue or Orange Line trolley to Civic Center.**

❶ ★ **Horton Plaza.** A colorful conglomeration of shops, eateries, and fanciful architecture, Horton Plaza spearheaded the revitalization of downtown when it opened in 1985. The ground floor is home to the Jessop Street Clock, designed by Joseph Jessop, Sr., and built primarily by Claude D. Ledger. It stood outside Jessop's Jewelry Store on Fifth Avenue from 1907 until being moved to Horton Plaza in 1985, and has reportedly only stopped three times in its history: once after being hit by a team of horses, once after an earthquake, and again on the day in 1935 when Ledger died. *Bound by Broadway, First, and Fourth aves., and G St.* ☎ *619/239-8180. www.westfield.com/hortonplaza.*

❷ **Horton Plaza Park.** Its centerpiece is a fountain designed by well-known local architect Irving Gill. It was dedicated October 15, 1910, and it was the first successful attempt to combine colored lights with flowing water. On the fountain's base are bronze medallions of San Diego's "founding fathers": Juan Rodríguez Cabrillo, Father Junípero Serra, and Alonzo Horton. *Corner of Fourth Ave. and Broadway.*

❸ ★ **Balboa Theatre.** Constructed in 1924, the Spanish Renaissance–style building has a distinctive tile dome, striking tile work in the entry, and two 20-foot-high (6m) ornamental waterfalls inside. In the theater's early days, plays and vaudeville took top billing. After years of sitting dormant and decrepit, the renovated Balboa is hosting live performances once again. *868 Fourth Ave. (southwest corner of Fourth Ave. and E St.).* ☎ *619/570-1100 or 619/615-4000. www.sdbalboa.org.*

❹ ★ **Watts-Robinson Building.** Built in 1913 in a Chicago School of Architecture style, this was one of San Diego's first skyscrapers. It once housed 70 jewelers and is now a boutique hotel (see Gaslamp Plaza Suites, p 137). Take a minute to look inside at the marble wainscoting, tile floors, ornate ceiling, and brass ornamentation. *903 Fifth Ave. (northeast corner of Fifth Ave. and E St.).*

❺ ★★ **Louis Bank of Commerce.** Built in 1888, this iconic building was the first in San Diego made of granite. It once housed the city's first ice-cream parlor; an oyster bar frequented by Wyatt Earp (of OK Corral shootout fame); and, upstairs, the Golden Poppy Hotel, a brothel run by a fortuneteller, Madame Coara. After a fire in 1904, the original towers of the building

Louis Bank.

were removed, and the iron eagles perched atop them disappeared. A 2002 renovation installed a new pair of eagles, cast at the same English foundry as the originals. *835 Fifth Ave.*

6 ★ Keating Building. A San Diego landmark dating from 1890, this structure was nicknamed the "marriage building." It was developed by businessman George Keating, who died halfway through construction; his wife, Fannie, finished the project, changing some of the design along the way. She had her husband's name engraved in the top cornice as a tribute to him.

The Keating Building at night.

Originally heralded as one of the city's most prestigious office buildings, it featured conveniences such as steam heat and a wire-cage elevator. A sleek boutique hotel, the Keating, is now ensconced here (see p 140). *432 F St. (northwest corner of Fifth Ave. and F St.).*

7 ★ Spencer-Ogden Building. Built in 1874, this is one of the oldest buildings in the Gaslamp Quarter—and it's lucky to still be standing. It escaped major damage after an explosion in 1887 caused by a druggist who was making fireworks. Other tenants over the years included realtors, an import business, a home-furnishing business, and a "Painless Parker" dental office. Edgar Parker owned a chain of dental offices and legally changed his name to "Painless" in order to avoid claims of false advertising. *770 Fifth Ave.*

8 ★ Old City Hall. Also dating from 1874, when it was a bank, this Florentine Italianate building features 16-foot (5m) ceilings, 12-foot (4m) windows framed with brick arches, antique columns, and a wrought-iron cage elevator. Notice that the windows on each floor are different. (The top two stories were

Touring the Town

Old Town Trolley Tours (☎ 619/298-8687; www.historictours.com) offer an easy way to get an overview of the city. These vehicles, gussied up like old-time trolleys, do a 30-mile (48km) circular route, and you can hop off at any one of 11 stops, explore at leisure, and reboard when you please (the trolleys run every half-hour). Stops include Old Town, the Gaslamp Quarter and downtown area, Coronado, the San Diego Zoo, and Balboa Park. You can begin wherever you want, but you must purchase tickets before boarding (most stops have a ticket kiosk). This narrated ride costs $32 for adults ($16 for kids 4–12, free for children 3 and under) for one complete circuit; the route by itself takes about 2 hours. The trolleys operate daily from 9am to 5pm in winter, and from 9am to 6pm in summer.

Vizit Tours (☎ 619/727-4007; www.vizitsandiegotours.com) features narrated tours aboard double-decker buses along four routes, including loops along the Harbor (which includes downtown), through Balboa Park, and up to Mission Beach and La Jolla. There are on-and-off privileges, and each tour is about an hour; you can also combine the routes into one city tour that also includes admission to the zoo (all tickets are valid for 48 hours). Most tours start in Seaport Village and run daily from 10am to 5pm; prices range from $15–$35 for adults, and $12–$29 for children.

added in 1887, when it became the city's public library.) The entire city government filled this building in 1900, with the police department on the first floor and the council chambers on the fourth. Incredibly, this beauty was completely encased in stucco in the 1950s in an attempt at modernization. It was restored in the 1980s. *664 Fifth Ave. (southwest corner of Fifth Ave. and G St.).*

9 ★★ Yuma Building. The striking edifice was built in 1888 and was one of the first brick buildings downtown. The brothel at the Yuma was the first to be closed during the infamous 1912 cleanup of the area. In the end, 138 women (and no men) were arrested. They were given a choice: Join the Door of Hope charity and reform or take a one-way train

ride to Los Angeles. One hundred thirty-six went to Los Angeles (many were back within days); one woman was pronounced insane; and the last

The Yuma Building.

became San Diego's first telephone operator. *631 Fifth Ave.*

⑩ ★ I.O.O.F. Building. Finally finished in 1882 after 9 years of construction, this handsome building served as a joint lodge for the Masons and Odd Fellows. Gaslamp lore has it that while watching a parade from the balcony, King Kalakaua, Hawaii's last reigning king, caught cold and died shortly thereafter in San Francisco in 1891. *526 Market St.*

⑪ Backesto Building. Built in 1873, this classical revival and Victorian corner building was expanded to its present size and height over its first 15 years. At the turn of the 20th century, this part of the Gaslamp was known as the Stingaree, the city's notorious red-light district. Gambling, opium dens, and wild saloons were all part of the mix. *617 Fifth Ave. (northwest corner of Fifth Ave. and Market St.).*

⑫ ★ William Heath Davis House. Downtown's oldest surviving structure, this prefabricated lumber home was shipped to San Diego around Cape Horn from New England in 1850. Alonzo Horton lived in the house in 1867, at its original location at the corner of Market and State streets. Around 1873 it was moved to 11th Avenue and K Street, where it served as the county hospital. It was relocated to this site in 1984, and completely refurbished. The entire house, now a museum and educational gift shop, and the small park next to it are open to the public (see p 39, bullet ⑧). The Gaslamp Quarter Historical Foundation is also headquartered here. *410 Island Ave. (at Fourth Ave.).* ☎ *619/233-4692. www.gaslampquarter.org.*

⑬ ★ Horton Grand Hotel. Two hotels, both built in 1886, were

The relocated historic Davis House.

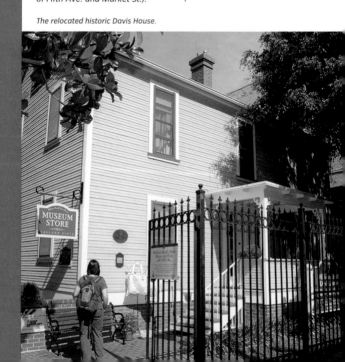

moved here—very gently—from other sites, and then renovated and connected by an atrium; the original Grand Horton is to your left, the Brooklyn Hotel to your right. Now it's all one: the Horton Grand Hotel (see p 139). The life-size papier-mâché horse (Sunshine), in the sitting area near reception, stood in front of the Brooklyn Hotel when the ground floor was a saddlery. Wyatt Earp lived upstairs at the Brooklyn for most of his 7 years in San Diego. In the Palace Bar, look for the portrait of Ida Bailey, a local madam whose establishment, the Canary Cottage, once stood nearby. *311 Island Ave. (southwest corner of Island and Fourth aves.).*

⑭ **Chinese Mission.** Originally on First Avenue, this charming brick building built in 1927 was a place where Chinese immigrants (primarily men) could learn English and find employment. Religious instruction and living quarters were also provided. The building was rescued from demolition and moved to its present location, where it now contains the San Diego Chinese Historical Museum. There's also a gift shop and a small garden. 🕐 *20 min. 404 Third Ave. (at J St.). ☎ 619/338-9888. www.sdchm.org. Admission $2 adults, free for children under 12. Tues–Sat 10:30am–4pm; Sun noon–4pm.*

⑮ **Brokers Building.** Constructed in 1889, this building has 16-foot (5m) wood-beam ceilings and cast-iron columns. In recent years it was converted to artists' lofts, with the ground floor dedicated to the downtown branch of the Hooters chain. Due to the failure of many previous ventures here, as well as a fire and a structural collapse, this was thought of as a "cursed corner." *402 Market St. (northeast corner of Fourth Ave. and Market St.).*

The Horton Grand.

It has a hip, bohemian vibe (hookah pipes are available), but if you're straight-arrow conservative, don't be put off— ⑯ **Café Lulu** is an inclusive place. Ostensibly a coffee bar, the cafe also serves sweets and has a full bar; it stays open late, too. *419 F St. (near Fourth Ave.). ☎ 619/238-0114. Sun–Thurs 11am–1am; Fri–Sat 11am–3am. $2–$8.*

⑰ ★ **Ingle Building.** It dates from 1906 and is now home to the Hard Rock Cafe. The mural on the F Street side of the building depicts a group of deceased rock stars (including Hendrix, Lennon, Joplin, and Elvis, of course) lounging at sidewalk tables. Stained-glass windows from the original Golden Lion Tavern (1907–32) front Fourth Avenue. Inside, the restaurant's stained-glass ceiling was taken from the Elks Club in Stockton, California, and much of the floor is original. *801 Fourth Ave. (northeast corner of Fourth Ave. and F St.).*

Old Town

1. McCoy House
2. Robinson-Rose House
3. Fiesta de Reyes
4. Large Rock Monument
5. La Casa de Estudillo
6. Colorado House
7. Mason Street School
8. Pedroreña House
9. San Diego Union Printing Office
10. Immaculate Conception Catholic Church
11. Living Room Cafe & Bistro
12. Whaley House
13. El Campo Santo
14. San Diego County Sheriff's Museum
15. Heritage Park

San Diego's Mexican and Spanish colonial history is vividly evident in Old Town. A visit here will transport you to an era of village greens and one-room schoolhouses, a time when *vaqueros* and whalers, outlaws and officers, *Californios* and Yankees all mingled— sometimes uneasily—in this then-tiny pueblo. When you stroll through Old Town State Historic Park, California's most popular state park, you don't have to look hard or very far to see a glimmer of yesteryear. This free park is just part of the Old Town experience, though. The compact neighborhood is home to other historic sites, as well as lots of shopping and dining, much of it themed to California's frontier past. START: **Blue or Green Line trolley to Old Town Transit Center.**

1 McCoy House. The interpretive center for Old Town State Historic Park (see p 9, bullet **2**) is a historically accurate replication of the home of James McCoy, San Diego's larger-than-life lawman/ legislator who lived on this site until the devastating fire of 1872. With exhibits, artifacts, and visitor information, the house gives a great

overview of life in San Diego from 1821 to 1872. ⏱ *30 min. Wallace and Calhoun sts. (northwest corner of the park).*

2 Robinson-Rose House. Built in 1853 as a family home, the park visitor center was also once a newspaper and railroad office. Here you'll see a large model of Old Town the way it looked prior to 1872—the year a large fire broke out and destroyed much of the town, initiating the exodus to what is now downtown San Diego. Old Town State Historic Park contains seven original buildings, including the Robinson-Rose House, and replicas of other buildings that once stood here. 🕐 *15 min.*

3 Fiesta de Reyes. Colorful shops and restaurants spill into a flower-filled courtyard where costumed employees and weekend entertainment create an early-California atmosphere. A motel in the 1930s, it was designed by acclaimed architect Richard Requa. 🕐 *30 min. Juan St. (btw. Wallace and Mason sts.).* ☎ *619/297-3100. www.fiesta dereyes.com.*

4 Large Rock Monument. This site commemorates the first U.S. flag flown in Southern California, hoisted here on July 29, 1846.

5 ★ La Casa de Estudillo. An original adobe building from 1827, this U-shaped house has covered walkways and an open central patio. The patio covering is made of corraza cane, grown from seeds brought by Father Serra in 1769. The walls are 3- to 5-feet (1- to 1.5m-) thick, holding up the heavy beams and tiles, and insulating

A Spanish tile staircase in Old Town.

against summer heat (in those days, the thicker the walls, the wealthier the family). The furnishings in this "upper-class" house are representative of the 19th century (note the beautiful four-poster beds); the original furniture came from as far away as the East Coast and even Asia. The Estudillo family, which then numbered 12, lived in the house until 1887; today family members still live in San Diego.

6 Colorado House. Built in 1851, it was destroyed by fire in 1872, as were most buildings on this side of the park. Now the home of the Wells Fargo Historical Museum, it originally was San Diego's first two-story hotel. The museum features an original Wells Fargo stagecoach, numerous displays of the

The road into Old Town.

Docents at La Casa de Estudillo.

overland-express business, and a video presentation. Next-door to the Wells Fargo museum, and kitty-corner to La Casa de Estudillo, is the small, redbrick San Diego Court House & City Hall. ⏱ **15 min.**

7 ★ **Mason Street School.** An original building dating from 1865, this school was commissioned by San Diego's first mayor, Joshua Bean, brother of the notorious "hanging judge" Roy Bean. Inside, you'll notice the boards that make up the walls don't match; they were leftovers from the construction of San Diego homes. Mary Chase Walker, the first teacher, ventured here from the East when she was 38 years old. She enjoyed the larger salary but hated the fleas, mosquitoes, and truancy; after a year, she

Inside the Mason St. School.

resigned to marry the president of the school board.

8 **Pedroreña House.** No. 2616 is an original Old Town house built in 1869, with stained glass over the doorway. The shop inside now sells fossils, minerals, and gems. The original owner, Miguel Pedroreña, a Spanish-born merchant and local bigwig, also owned the house next door.

9 **San Diego Union Printing Office.** This house arrived in Old Town after being prefabricated in Maine in 1851 and shipped around the Horn (it has a distinctly New England–style appearance). Inside you'll see the original hand press used to print the *San Diego Union*, first published out of this building in 1868. The *Union* merged with the *San Diego Tribune* in 1992; the *Union-Tribune* remains San Diego's newspaper of record.

10 **Immaculate Conception Catholic Church.** The cornerstone was laid in 1868, making it the first church built in California that was not part of the Mission system. With the movement of the community to New Town in 1872, it lost its parishioners and wasn't dedicated until 1919. Today the church serves about 300 families in the Old Town area. *2540 San Diego Ave. (at Twiggs St., which divides the park*

Old Town's Heritage Park.

from the rest of Old Town). ☎ 619/
295-4148. www.ic-sandiego.org.

Grab a patio table in the courtyard
of the lovely ⑪ **Living Room
Cafe & Bistro** and enjoy the peo-
ple- watching, as well as light meals
for breakfast, lunch, or dinner. *2541
San Diego Ave.* ☎ *619/325-4445.
www.livingroomcafe.com. Sun–
Thurs 7am–10pm; Fri–Sat 7am–midnight. $6–$10.*

⑫ **Whaley House.** The first two-
story brick structure in Southern California, it was built between 1856 and
1857. The house is said to be
haunted by several ghosts, including
that of Yankee Jim Robinson, who
was hanged on the site in 1852 for
stealing a rowboat. The house is
beautifully furnished with period
pieces and also features the life mask
of Abraham Lincoln. The home's
north room served as the county
courthouse for a few years, and the
courtroom looks now as it did then.
🕐 *30 min. See p 35, bullet* ②.

⑬ **El Campo Santo.** Behind an
adobe wall along San Diego Avenue
is San Diego's first cemetery, established in 1850. This small plot is the
final resting place for, among others, the unfortunate Yankee Jim

Robinson (see above). Note the
small, round brass markers along
the sidewalk and in the street. They
mark the still-buried remains of
some of San Diego's earliest citizens, unknown souls paved over by
the tide of progress. *Two short
blocks south of the Whaley House on
the east side of San Diego Ave.*

⑭ **San Diego County Sheriff's
Museum.** Exhibits trace the evolu-
tion of the department and its
equipment since San Diego sheriffs
first pinned a badge on in 1850. The
building itself is a stone's throw
from where the city's original cob-
blestone jail once stood. 🕐 *20 min.
2384 San Diego Ave.* ☎ *619/260-
1850. www.sheriffmuseum.org. Free
admission. Tues–Sat 10am–4pm.*

⑮ **Heritage Park.** Seven original
19th-century buildings are in this
8-acre (3.2-hectare) park; each was
saved from destruction and moved
here from another part of the city.
Among the highlights are the Sher-
man-Gilbert House (1887), with its
distinctive widow's walk, and the
classic revival Temple Beth Israel,
dating from 1889. These structures
will be joined by a new bed-and-
breakfast village with Victorian-style
buildings. *2450 Heritage Park Row
(corner of Juan and Harney sts.). See
p 35, bullet* ②.

Embarcadero

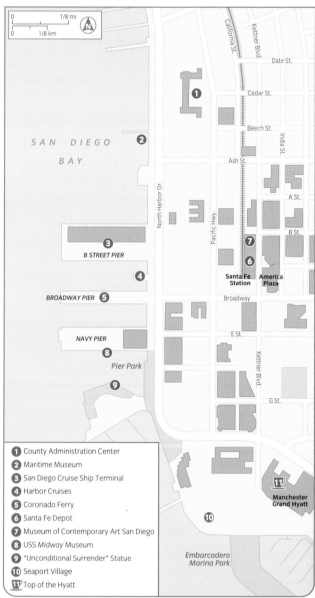

1 County Administration Center
2 Maritime Museum
3 San Diego Cruise Ship Terminal
4 Harbor Cruises
5 Coronado Ferry
6 Santa Fe Depot
7 Museum of Contemporary Art San Diego
8 USS *Midway* Museum
9 "Unconditional Surrender" Statue
10 Seaport Village
11 Top of the Hyatt

Upon seeing San Diego Bay in 1602, the second European visitor to the area, Sebastián Vizcaíno, declared it to be "a port which must be the best to be found in all the South Sea." A walk along the waterfront, known as the Embarcadero, may convince you as well. Whalers, merchants with goods from Asia, and tanners (San Diego is the location of "Hide Park" in Richard Henry Dana's *Two Years Before the Mast*) made San Diego Bay a mid-19th century commercial hub. Up until the 1950s, the world's biggest tuna fleet was here, too. While things may be a little more genteel along the Embarcadero now than they were in 1850—tourism is the main commerce these days—it's still a world-class harbor. START: **Blue Line trolley to County Center/Little Italy.**

1 County Administration Center.
Built in 1936 with funds from the Works Progress Administration, the center was dedicated in 1938 by President Franklin D. Roosevelt. This Art Deco beauty is one of San Diego's most graceful buildings and is listed on the National Register of Historic Places. The waterfront side is presided over by the dignified 23-foot-high (7m) granite statue, *Guardian of Water,* created by San Diego's most notable sculptor, Donal Hord. A cafeteria with great harbor views is on the fourth floor. *1600 Pacific Hwy.* ☎ *619/531-5197. Mon–Fri 8am–5pm.*

2 ★★ kids Maritime Museum.
Not a building but a collection of ships, the main attraction is the magnificent *Star of India,* built in 1863. It's the world's oldest ship that still puts to sea. The vessel, whose billowing sails are a familiar sight along Harbor Drive, once carried cargo to India, immigrants to New Zealand, and braved the Arctic ice in Alaska to work in the salmon industry. Another component of the museum is the 1898 ferry *Berkeley,* which operated between San Francisco and Oakland. In service through 1958, it carried survivors to safety 24 hours a day for 4 days after the 1906 San Francisco earthquake. You can also check out the HMS *Surprise,* which had a star turn in the film *Master and Commander;* a Soviet-era B-39 attack submarine; the *Californian,* a replica of a 19th-century revenue cutter; the *Medea,* a 1904 steam yacht; and the *Pilot,* which served as San Diego Bay's official pilot boat for 82 years. See p 38, bullet 7.

Downtown San Diego's Marriott marina near Seaport Village.

The Maritime Museum of San Diego.

③ San Diego Cruise Ship Terminal. Located on the B Street Pier, it has a large nautical clock at the entrance. The flag-decorated terminal's interior is light and airy; you'll also find a snack bar, gift shop, and restrooms.

④ ★ Harbor Cruises. Hornblower Cruises and San Diego Harbor Excursions run daily 1- and 2-hour sightseeing cruises around the bay, departing from near the Broadway Pier. Choose from a variety of vessels, everything from antique yachts to three-deck behemoths, and both companies also offer evening dinner/dance cruises, as well as weekend Champagne brunch packages. Ticket booths are right along the waterfront. *Hornblower Cruises* ☎ 888/467-6256 or

Richard Serra sculptures at the Museum of Contemporary Art San Diego.

619/686-8715. www.hornblower. com. Harbor tours $20–$25 adults, $2 off for seniors and military, half price children 4–12. Dinner cruises start at $70; brunch cruise $53. San Diego Harbor Excursions ☎ *800/442-7847 or 619/234-4111. www.sdhe. com. Harbor tours $20–$25 ($2 off for seniors and military, half price for children 4–12). Dinner cruises start at $67 adults, $38 children; brunch cruise $55 adults, $38 children.*

⑤ Coronado Ferry. This pedestrian-only ferry makes hourly trips between San Diego and Coronado. Buy tickets from the Harbor Excursion booth—a one-way trip is 15 minutes. *Sun–Thurs on the hour from 9am–9pm, Fri–Sat till 10pm. Return trips from the Ferry Landing in Coronado to the Broadway Pier are Sun–Thurs every hour on the half-hour from 9:30am–9:30pm, Fri–Sat till 10:30pm. $3.50 each way.*

⑥ ★ Santa Fe Depot. This mosaic-draped railroad station was built in 1915, and provides one of the city's best examples of Spanish Colonial Revival style. Check out the vaulted ceiling, wooden benches, and walls covered in striking green-and-gold tiles. A scale model of the aircraft carrier USS *Midway* is also on display. *West end of Broadway btw. India St. and Kettner Blvd.*

7 ★★★ **Museum of Contemporary Art San Diego.** What was once the train station's baggage building has been transformed into a dynamic space for this cutting-edge art museum. Designed by the same architect responsible for the Warhol museum in Pittsburgh and the Picasso museum in Spain, this is one of the city's cultural flagships, featuring permanent, site-specific work by artists such as Richard Serra and Jenny Holzer. Changing exhibitions are scheduled at both this space and MCASD's original downtown annex across the street. ⏱ *1 hr. 1100 and 1001 Kettner Blvd. (between B St. and Broadway).* ☎ *858/454-3541. www.mcasd.org. Admission $10 adults, $5 seniors and military, free for anyone 25 and under, free admission 3rd Thurs 5–7pm; paid ticket good for admission to MCASD La Jolla within 7 days. Thurs–Tues 11am–5pm; 3rd Thurs 11am–7pm.*

8 **USS *Midway* Museum.** Decommissioned in 1991, the USS *Midway* saw 47 years of service, stretching from the end of World War II to Desert Storm, where it acted as the flagship for that operation. This aircraft carrier is now a floating naval museum, telling the story of life on board during its missions. *See p 38, bullet* **6**.

9 **"Unconditional Surrender" Statue.** Kitsch on a giant scale. This 25-foot, full-color statue re-creates an iconic American image: Alfred Eisenstaedt's 1945 photo of a sailor and nurse in passionate embrace following the news of Japan's surrender in World War II. Nearby is a salute to another American icon, Bob Hope. Featuring a cast of 15 bronze statues, this installation depicts the comedian entertaining the troops.

10 **kids** **Seaport Village.** This 14-acre (5.6-hectare) outdoor shopping center has more than 50 stores and restaurants, coupled with an unbeatable bayfront location. Kids love the classic carousel—Charles Looff of Coney Island carved the animals out of poplar in 1895; live entertainment is also often scheduled on weekends. *849 W. Harbor Dr. (at Kettner Blvd.).* ☎ *619/235-4014. www. seaportvillage.com. Daily 10am–9pm; restaurants have extended hours.*

There's no better place in San Diego for a sunset than the **11** ★★ **Top of the Hyatt,** a 40th-floor lounge with sweeping views of the city and harbor. It's in the eastern tower of the Manchester Grand Hyatt and opens at 3pm daily. *1 Market Pl.* ☎ *619/232-1234. $5–$15.*

The San Diego Pier Café at Seaport Village.

La Jolla

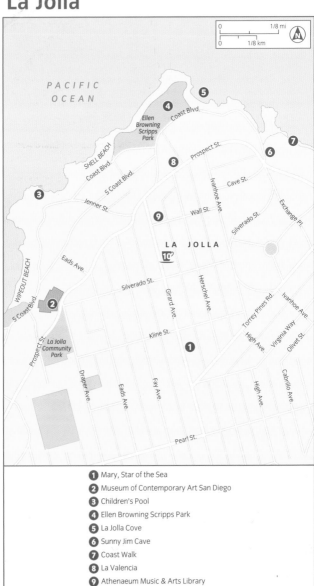

PACIFIC
OCEAN

Ellen Browning Scripps Park

SHELL BEACH

WIPEOUT BEACH

La Jolla Community Park

LA JOLLA

Coast Blvd.
S Coast Blvd.
Jenner St.
Eads Ave.
S Coast Blvd.
Prospect St.
Draper Ave.
Eads Ave.
Fay Ave.
Girard Ave.
Kline St.
Silverado St.
Wall St.
Prospect St.
Ivanhoe Ave.
Cave St.
Silverado St.
Herschel Ave.
High Ave.
Torrey Pines Rd.
High Ave.
Virginia Way
Olivet St.
Cabrillo Ave.
Ivanhoe Ave.
Exchange Pl.
Pearl St.

1 Mary, Star of the Sea
2 Museum of Contemporary Art San Diego
3 Children's Pool
4 Ellen Browning Scripps Park
5 La Jolla Cove
6 Sunny Jim Cave
7 Coast Walk
8 La Valencia
9 Athenaeum Music & Arts Library
10 Girard Gourmet

La Jolla is Southern California's Riviera. This seaside community of about 25,000 is home to an inordinate number of wealthy folk who could probably live anywhere. They choose La Jolla for good reason—it features a gorgeous coastline, outstanding restaurants, and a slew of upscale boutiques and galleries. The heart of La Jolla is referred to as the Village, roughly delineated by Pearl Street to the south, Prospect Street to the north, Torrey Pines Road to the east, and the rugged coast to the west; this picturesque neighborhood is an ideal place to simply stroll about. It's undetermined whether "La Jolla" (pronounced la-HOY-ya) is misspelled Spanish for "the jewel" or an indigenous word for "cave," but once you see it, you'll likely go with the first definition. START: **Bus route 30 to Silverado St. and Girard Ave.**

① ★ Mary, Star of the Sea. Dedicated in 1937, this beautiful little Mission-style Catholic church was designed by noted San Diego architect Carleton Winslow, Sr. Above the entrance, a striking mosaic re-creates the original fresco painted there by Mexican artist Alfredo Ramos Martínez. An influential art instructor in Mexico, Martínez's students included Rufino Tamayo and David Alfaro Siqueiros. Inside the church, the unique mural above the altar was painted by accomplished Polish artist John De Rosen. It depicts the Virgin Mary on a crescent moon, presiding over a storm-tossed sea. ⏱ *15 min. 7669 Girard Ave.* ☎ *858/454-2631. www. marystarlajolla.org. Mon–Fri 6am– noon and daily services.*

② ★★★ Museum of Contemporary Art San Diego. Focusing on work produced since 1950, this museum's holdings include noteworthy examples of minimalism, light and space work, conceptualism, installation, and site-specific art (the outside sculptures were designed specifically for this location). MCASD also offers lectures, cutting-edge films, and special events on an ongoing basis; the bookstore is a great place for contemporary gifts, and the cafe is a pleasant stop before or after your visit. The museum is on a bluff overlooking the Pacific Ocean, and the views from the galleries are gorgeous. The original building on the site, designed by Irving Gill in 1916, was the residence of Ellen Browning

An Andy Goldsworthy sculpture at the Museum of Contemporary Art San Diego.

MUSEUM OF
CONTEMPORARY

Scripps. ⏲ *90 min. 700 Prospect St.* ☎ *858/454-3541. www.mcasd.org. Admission $10 adults, $5 seniors, students, and military, free for ages 25 and under; free 3rd Thurs of the month 5–7pm; paid ticket good for admission to MCASD downtown within 7 days. Thurs–Tues 11am–5pm; 3rd Thurs 11am–7pm.*

③ ★★ kids Children's Pool. A seawall protects this pocket of sand—originally intended as a calm swimming bay for children, but serving since 1994 as a sanctuary for a colony of harbor seals; on an average day you'll spot dozens lolling in the sun. After much heated debate (and even acts of civil disobedience), people were allowed to swim here again—to the displeasure of many. While it is possible to now go in the water at the Children's Pool, keep in mind those are federally protected *wild* animals, and it is illegal to approach them or harass them in any way. The water here can also have high levels of bacteria, so content yourself with viewing the animals from a safe distance. Also note that volunteers, with speed dials set to "lifeguard," keep watch to make sure no one bothers the colony.

④ ★★ Ellen Browning Scripps Park. This park and the bluff-side walkway that courses through it afford some of California's finest coastal scenery. There's plenty of soft grass where you can toss a Frisbee, have a picnic, or just laze. A series of rustic wooden shelters—popular among seagulls, pigeons, and pedestrians—overlooks La Jolla's shapely curves. The La Jolla Cove Bridge Club—a Works Project Administration structure dating to 1939, where card games still take place—must be one of the world's most view-enhanced card rooms. *La Jolla Cove Bridge Club.* ☎ *858/459-7000. www.lajollacovebridge club.org. Games Sun, Wed, and Fri noon–3:30pm.*

⑤ ★★★ kids La Jolla Cove. These protected calm waters, celebrated as the clearest along the coast, attract snorkelers, scuba divers, and families. The small sandy beach gets a bit cramped during the summer, but the cove's "look but don't touch" policy safeguards the colorful garibaldi, California's state marine fish, plus other sea life, including abalone, octopus, and lobster. The unique Underwater Park stretches from here to the northern end of Torrey Pines State Reserve and incorporates kelp forests, artificial reefs, two deep canyons, and tidal pools.

The coast walk at Boomer Beach.

The Athenaeum library.

6 **kids** **Sunny Jim Cave.** The only one of La Jolla's seven sea caves accessible by land, the Sunny Jim Cave is reached by a narrow, often slippery, staircase in the Cave Store. (Sunny Jim was a cartoon character created in 1902 for a cereal advertising campaign, and the cave opening resembles his profile.) Part art gallery, part antiques store, this cliff-top shop also rents snorkel equipment. The passageway with 145 steps was dug through the rock in 1902–03. 🕐 *20 min. 1325 Cave St. (just off Prospect St.).* ☎ *858/459-0746. www.cavestore. com. $4 adults, $3 kids 3–16, free for 2 and under. Daily 9am–5pm.*

7 ★★ **Coast Walk.** As you face the ocean, continue past the Cave Store. You'll find two paths; one leads to a fabulous wood-platform overlook, the other continues along the bluffs. It's a cool little trail, affording expansive views of the coast. You can exit at a stairway that leads back to Prospect Street (before you come to the white wooden bridge) and circle back into town. If you continue along the trail, it will put you on Torrey Pines Road, an extra 10- to 15-minute walk back to the village.

8 ★★★ **La Valencia.** Within its bougainvillea-draped walls and wrought-iron garden gates, this bastion of gentility resurrects a golden age, when celebrities like Greta Garbo and Charlie Chaplin vacationed here. The blufftop hotel, which looks much like a Mediterranean villa, has been the centerpiece of La Jolla since opening in 1926. Among the several lounges and restaurants, some have incredible vistas, which can be enjoyed by nonguests; the Whaling Bar is a classic, old-school haunt (see p 15, bullet **5**). 🕐 *15 min. 1132 Prospect St. (at Herschel Ave.).*

☎ *800/451-0772 or 858/454-0771. www.lavalencia.com.*

9 ★★ **Athenaeum Music & Arts Library.** One of only 16 non-profit, membership libraries in the U.S., the Athenaeum hosts art exhibits, jazz and classical concerts, lectures, and special events open to the general public. Visitors can browse through the vast collection of books, music, and more, but only members can take something out. Founded in 1899, the library has expanded into adjacent buildings, including one built by Balboa Park architect William Templeton Johnson. 🕐 *30 min. 1008 Wall St. (at Girard Ave.).* ☎ *858/454-5872. www. ljathenaeum.org. Gallery exhibits are free. Tues and Thurs–Sat 10am–5:30pm; Wed 10am–8:30pm.*

With its small bakery and restaurant, **10** ★ **Girard Gourmet** always draws a crowd for its cookies, quiches, soups, salads, and deli sandwiches (the eight-grain bread is a must). The Belgian proprietor also whips up heartier fare like lamb stew and duck *à l'orange.* It's the perfect place to gather your goods for a picnic. *7837 Girard Ave.* ☎ *858/454-3325. www.girard gourmet.com. Mon–Sat 7am–8pm; Sun 7am–7pm. $2–$22.*

Hillcrest

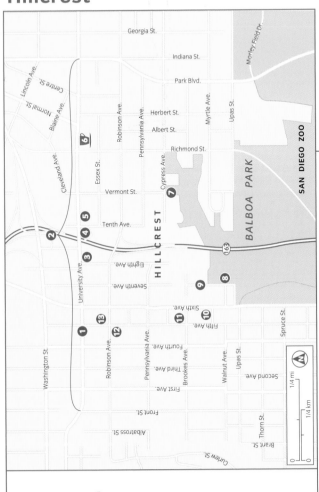

Georgia St.

Indiana St.

Park Blvd.

Morley Field Dr.

Lincoln Ave.

Centre St.

Normal St.

Blaine Ave.

Herbert St.

Albert St.

Robinson Ave.

Pennsylvania Ave.

Richmond St.

Myrtle Ave.

Upas St.

SAN DIEGO ZOO

Cleveland Ave.

Essex St.

Cypress Ave.

Vermont St.

BALBOA PARK

Tenth Ave.

⑤ ④

⑥

⑦

② ③

Eighth Ave.

Seventh Ave.

HILLCREST

163

University Ave.

⑧

⑨

Sixth Ave.

⑬

① ⑫

⑪ ⑩

Fifth Ave.

Spruce St.

Washington St.

Robinson Ave.

Pennsylvania Ave.

Fourth Ave.

Third Ave.

Brookes Ave.

Walnut Ave.

Upas St.

Second Ave.

First Ave.

Front St.

Albatross St.

Brant St.

Thorn St.

Curlew St.

1/4 mi
1/4 km

- ❶ Hillcrest Sign
- ❷ "Fossils Exposed"
- ❸ House of Heirlooms
- ❹ "The Loading Dock"
- ❺ John Wear Memorial
- ❻ Mamá Testa Taqueria
- ❼ Marston Addition Canyon
- ❽ Marston House
- ❾ Seventh Avenue
- ❿ Wednesday Club
- ⓫ Design Center
- ⓬ Brass Rail
- ⓭ Guild Theater

Centrally located and brimming with popular restaurants and boutiques, Hillcrest is one of San Diego's most vibrant neighborhoods, thanks in no small part to its role as the heart of the local gay and lesbian community. In the 1920s, Hillcrest was the city's first self-contained suburb, making it a desirable address for bankers and businessmen, who built their mansions here. Despite the cachet of being close to Balboa Park (home of the San Diego Zoo and numerous museums), the area fell into neglect in the 1960s. By the late 1970s, however, legions of preservation-minded residents began restoring Hillcrest, and the community is once again among San Diego's best places to live, work, and play. START: **Bus route 1, 3, or 120 to Fifth and University aves.**

1 Hillcrest Sign. Donated to the community in 1940 by a group of local businesswomen, this Art Deco Hillcrest landmark stretches 21 feet (6.5m) across University Avenue, utilizing 240 feet (73m) of pink neon lighting. It went dark for some time, but was taken down and refurbished in 1983. Its relighting in August 1984 was the genesis for Hillcrest's annual street fair. Also of note, on the north side of University, is the neon sign for Jimmy Wong's Golden Dragon, a holdover from 1955 (the restaurant itself is defunct). *Corner of University and Fifth aves.*

2 "Fossils Exposed." You can go on a bit of a scavenger hunt as you walk the neighborhood, searching for artist Doron Rosenthal's "Fossils Exposed." This 1998 public art project features 150 granite markers randomly embedded into the sidewalk along University Avenue, from First Avenue to Park Boulevard. The 4½-inch (11cm) pieces are stylized representations of actual plant and animal fossils that would be found in this region.

3 House of Heirlooms. Built in 1919, this building was an antiques store for many years, but originally served as a surgery annex for St. Joseph's Sanitarium, a hospital opened by the Sisters of Mercy in 1891. Initially located across the street, it was moved to its present site in 1924, several years after the sisters relocated the hospital a few blocks away, where it continues to serve the community under the name Scripps Mercy Hospital. Preservationists were able to have the structure designated as historical in 2007, but it was a short-lived victory. In a tactic all-too-familiar in San Diego, the developer who now owns the property is allowing the building to decay until it becomes necessary to demolish it. *801 University Ave.*

4 "The Loading Dock." This detailed, trompe l'oeil mural was painted by artist Linda Churchill in 1999. *Corner of University and 10th aves.*

Hillcrest's Art Deco landmark sign.

Marston Addition Canyon.

⑤ John Wear Memorial. On December 13, 1991, 17-year-old John Wear was accosted and stabbed to death as he walked down the street with two friends because his assailants believed he was gay. This small plaque in the sidewalk in front of The Obelisk bookstore is dedicated to his memory and to the ending of all hate crimes. *1029 University Ave.*

⑥ ★★ Mamá Testa Taqueria features a nearly overwhelming selection of tacos—soft, rolled, or hard-shell—featuring recipes from all over Mexico. You won't find better tacos anywhere, on either side of the border. *1417A University Ave.* ☎ *619/298-8226. www.mama testataqueria.com. Mon–Thurs 11:30am–9pm; Fri–Sat 11:30am–11pm; Sun noon–8pm. $5–$9.*

⑦ ★ Marston Addition Canyon. Turn south down Vermont Street from University Avenue and head through part of residential Hillcrest. At the corner of Cypress Street, you'll come to the trail head for this open-space oasis in the heart of the city. Follow the (usually) dry creek bed toward the sound of the ocean—actually it's the traffic on Highway 163. Take the footbridge over the freeway and head up the paved path into Balboa Park proper. ⏰ *20 min.* **Note:** This is a very isolated part of the park. It's not recommended you attempt this after dark. If you are doing this walk in the evening, retrace your steps back to University and Sixth avenues, and resume the tour there.

⑧ ★ Marston House. Built in 1905, this gorgeous Craftsman mansion designed by William Hebbard and Irving Gill was the home of one of San Diego's most prominent families. It's now a museum sitting on 5 beautifully landscaped acres (2 hectares) and the interior is filled with decor and furniture from the Arts and Crafts period. *See p 39, bullet* ⑩.

⑨ ★ Seventh Avenue. Architecture buffs should continue on down Seventh Avenue for a concentrated dose of classic design. The 10 other houses on this short, shady street represent more brilliant work from

The George and Anna Marston House, on the National Register of Historic Places.

The neighborhood of Hillcrest, northwest of Balboa Park.

architects Irving Gill and William Hebbard, who created the Marston House, as well as prominent San Diego architects Richard Requa and Frank Mead. All the homes were constructed between 1905 and 1913 in what was known as Critten-den's Addition, which dates back to 1887. *Note:* These are all private residences, so keep to the sidewalk. *3500 block of Seventh Ave.*

⓾ **Wednesday Club.** With the encouragement of architect Irving Gill, Hazel Waterman pursued a career in architecture following the death of her husband, who was the son of California governor Robert Waterman. With her only formal architectural education coming via a correspondence course, Gill hired her on and she helped with three of the houses on Seventh Avenue (see above). She moved on to design this structure in 1911, clearly influenced by Gill. *540 Ivy Lane (Sixth Ave. and Ivy Lane).*

⓫ **Design Center.** Fans of con-temporary design will appreciate this building by architect Lloyd Ruocco, San Diego's leading post-war modernist. Built in 1949, the structure served as Ruocco's office and as the location of his wife Ilse's interior decorating business and showroom. Fittingly, the space has been used by a succession of archi-tectural and design firms ever since. *3611 Fifth Ave.*

⓬ **Brass Rail.** This is San Diego's oldest gay bar—it's been in the neighborhood since 1963 (although it was originally on the other side of the street, and prior to that, had been downtown). It's been in this spot since 1973. *3796 Fifth Ave. (at Robinson St.).* ☎ *619/298-2233. www.thebrassrailsd.com.*

⓭ **Guild Theater.** A series of failed enterprises has occupied what was once a beautiful, Spanish Revival–style movie house that first opened in 1913. Renamed the Guild in the late 1950s, the plug was finally pulled on it in 1997. A tragic event for many locals, the Guild was com-pletely destroyed—what you see is a re-creation of the facade based on the original design. *3835 Fifth Ave.*

Coronado

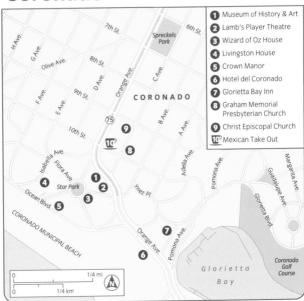

1 Museum of History & Art
2 Lamb's Player Theatre
3 Wizard of Oz House
4 Livingston House
5 Crown Manor
6 Hotel del Coronado
7 Glorietta Bay Inn
8 Graham Memorial Presbyterian Church
9 Christ Episcopal Church
10 Mexican Take Out

You may be tempted to think of Coronado as an island, but it's actually on a peninsula connected to the mainland by a narrow sand spit, the Silver Strand. It's a wealthy, self-contained community inhabited by lots of retired Navy brass who live on quiet, tree-lined streets. The northern portion of Coronado is home to a U.S. Naval base, in use since World War I; the rest of the area has a history as an elite playground for snowbirds with plenty of big, beautiful homes. Shops and restaurants line the main street, Orange Avenue, which is reminiscent of a Midwestern town. You'll also find several ritzy resorts, including the landmark Hotel del Coronado, which fronts one of the area's finest beaches. START: **Bus route 901.**

1 **Museum of History and Art.** This museum displays archival materials about the development of Coronado, as well as offering tourist information. Exhibits include photographs of the Hotel Del in its infancy, the old ferries, Tent City (a seaside campground for middle-income vacationers from 1900 to 1939), and notable residents and visitors. Other memorabilia include army uniforms,

old postcards, and even recorded music. You'll also learn about the island's military aviation history during World War I and II. ⏱ *30 min.* *1100 Orange Ave.* ☎ *619/435-7242.* *www.coronadohistory.org. Suggested donation $4 adults, $3 seniors and military, $2 youths 9–18, free for children 8 and under. Mon–Fri 9am–5pm; Sat–Sun 10am–5pm.*

② ★ Lamb's Player Theatre.

This acclaimed troupe is one of the few professional theaters in the country with a year-round resident company. They perform a wide range of work, from classics to new musicals. The intimate theater space is in the heart of a Neoclassical structure known as the Spreckels Building. Constructed of reinforced concrete in 1917, it was designed by Harrison Albright, who also created the Organ Pavilion in Balboa Park and the downtown Spreckels Theater at the behest of sugar magnates John and A. B. Spreckels. *1142 Orange Ave.* ☎ *619/437-0600. www.lambsplayers.org.*

③ Wizard of Oz House. Author

L. Frank Baum was a frequent visitor to Coronado, where he wrote several of his beloved Wizard of Oz books. It's believed he even patterned elements of the Emerald City after the architecture of the Hotel del Coronado. Baum occupied this colonial revival home, known as the Lemeche-Meade House, in the early 1900s. *Note:* This is a private home. *1101 Star Park Circle.*

④ ★★ Livingston House. Also

known as the Baby Del, this spectacular Queen Anne Revival home was

The Coronado Bridge.

originally located across the bay in San Diego. After 6 months of planning, it was moved to Coronado in 1983 for a cost of $120,000. Built in 1887, 6 months before the Hotel Del, it's believed the house was a training ground for carpenters who would work on the Del, and indeed, might have been designed by the Del's architects, working under a pseudonym. The house is privately owned, but has its own website. *1144 Isabella Ave. www.babydel.com.*

⑤ ★★ Crown Manor. San

Diego's all-star architectural team of William Hebbard and Irving Gill created the original designs for this amazing 27-bedroom, oceanfront estate in 1902. Also known as the

The Coronado Ferry Landing gate.

Richards-Dupee Mansion, this private home covers 20,000 square feet (1,858 sq. m) and was commissioned by Bartlett Richards, a Nebraska cattle baron. Richards ran afoul of the law for questionable land schemes in his home state and died while in federal custody in 1911. He was elected to the National Cowboy Hall of Fame in 1970. *1015 Ocean Blvd.*

⑥ ★★★ Hotel del Coronado.

San Diego's romantic Hotel del Coronado is an unmistakable landmark with a colorful past. When it opened in 1888, it was among the first buildings rigged with Thomas Edison's new invention, electric light (its electrical power plant supplied the entire city of Coronado until 1922). Author L. Frank Baum, a frequent guest, designed the dining room's original crown-shaped chandeliers. The hotel has also played host to royalty and celebrities—Edward, Prince of Wales (later King Edward VIII, and then Duke of Windsor), caused a sensation with his visit in 1920, and of course, Marilyn Monroe, Tony Curtis, and Jack Lemmon famously frolicked here in the film *Some Like It Hot. See p 18, bullet* ④.

⑦ ★★ Glorietta Bay Inn.

The Spreckels Mansion is now known as the Glorietta Bay Inn. It was designed by John Spreckels' go-to architect, Harrison Albright, and built in 1908.

The iconic Hotel del Coronado.

Spreckels, along with his family and money, abandoned San Francisco after the 1906 earthquake and set up shop in San Diego. He was particularly involved with Coronado, where he became sole owner of the Hotel Del. The Glorietta Bay Inn's 1950s motel-style annexes are lamentable, but the home's glory is still very much in evidence. *1630 Glorietta Blvd.* ☎ 800/283-9383 or 619/435-3101. www.gloriettabayinn.com.

⑧ ★ Graham Memorial Presbyterian Church.

The founding fathers of Coronado were land speculators who purchased the peninsula—mostly inhabited by jack rabbits—for $110,000 in 1885. Their intent from the beginning was to create a resort community. This lovely little church was built by Hotel Del architect James Reid for one of those original investors, Elisha S. Babcock, Jr., in 1890. The church was then dedicated to the memory of Babcock's in-laws, John and Susan Graham. *975 C Ave.*

⑨ ★ Christ Episcopal Church.

James and Watson Reid, the brother architects who created the Hotel del Coronado, designed this Gothic stone church. Completed in 1894, it features stained glass made by noted California artist, writer, and landscape designer Bruce Porter. The church was commissioned by Captain Charles Hinde (the magnificent Kirk-Hinde residence, also designed by the Reid brothers, is across the street at 959 C Ave.). *900 C Ave.*

The no-frills, walk-in-closet–sized ⑩ **Mexican Take Out** (yes, that's actually the name) lacks any pretense of charm, which of course is its charm. No eating on the premises. *1107 10th St. (at Orange Ave., behind Clayton's Coffee Shop).* ☎ 619/437-8811. Daily 11am–7pm. Cash only. $3–$8. ●

Shopping **Best Bets**

Best **Jewelry That Doubles as Art**
★★★ Taboo Studio 1615½ W. Lewis St. (p 79)

Best **Sexy Beachwear**
★★ Sauvage 1025 Prospect St. (p 77)

Best **Urban-Fabulous Sneakers**
★★ Mint 525 University Ave. (p 77)

Best **Vintage Clothing**
★★★ Wear It Again Sam 3823 Fifth Ave. (p 77)

Best **Spot for Local Artists**
★ Spanish Village Art Center 1770 Village Pl. (p 75)

Best **Place to Find Dr. Seuss on the Loose**
★★ Chuck Jones Gallery 232 Fifth Ave. (p 75)

Best **Place to Find Your Bearings**
★★★ Ruderman Antique Maps 7463 Girard Ave. (p 74)

Best **Place for Mid-Century Modernists**
★★★ Boomerang for Modern 2475 Kettner Blvd. (p 78); and ★★★ Mid-Century 3795 Park Blvd. (p 78)

Best **Fashions for Moms-to-Be**
★★ Baby Mabel's 136 S. Cedros Ave. (p 76)

Best **Denim**
★★ G-Star Raw 470 Fifth Ave. (p 76)

Best **Pop Culture Gifts**
★ Babette Schwartz 421 University Ave. (p 77)

Best **Stuff From Out of Africa**
★★ Africa and Beyond 1250 Prospect St. (p 74)

Best **Place to Buy a Trilobite**
★★ Dinosaur Gallery 1327 Camino del Mar (p 77)

Best **Beeswax**
★★ Knorr Candle Shop 14906 Villa de la Valle (p 78)

Best **Funky Bookstore**
★★ D.G. Wills Books 7461 Girard Ave. (p 75)

Best **Place for Rare Vinyl**
★★★ Folk Arts Rare Records 2881 Adams Ave. (p 79)

Best **Place for Surfer Girls and Boys**
★★ Quiksilver/Roxy 1111 Prospect St. (p 76)

Best **Greek Gods**
★★ Column One 401 University Ave. (p 78)

Best **Shopping Center for Fashionistas**
★★ Fashion Valley Center 7007 Friars Rd. (p 79)

Best **Shopping Center for Fashionistas Looking for Discounts**
★★★ Carlsbad Premium Outlets 5600 Paseo del Norte (p 79)

Previous page: DG Wills Books.

Downtown Shopping

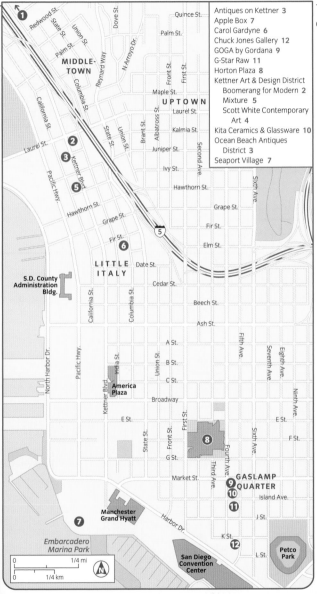

Antiques on Kettner 3
Apple Box 7
Carol Gardyne 6
Chuck Jones Gallery 12
GOGA by Gordana 9
G-Star Raw 11
Horton Plaza 8
Kettner Art & Design District
 Boomerang for Modern 2
 Mixture 5
 Scott White Contemporary
  Art 4
Kita Ceramics & Glassware 10
Ocean Beach Antiques
 District 3
Seaport Village 7

Hillcrest Shopping

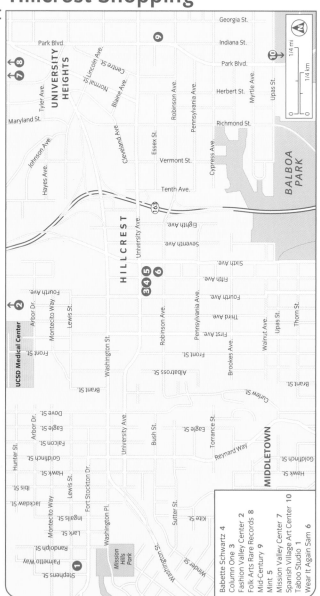

La Jolla Shopping

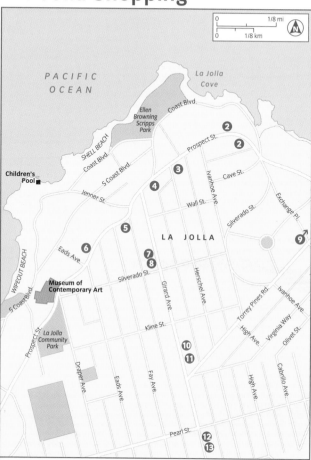

Africa and Beyond **2**
Blondstone **5**
D.G. Wills Books **13**
Emilia Castillo **1**
Joseph Bellows Gallery **10**
Laura Gambucci **11**
My Own Space **7**
Quiksilver/Roxy **3**
Ruderman Antique Maps **12**
Sauvage **4**
Tasende Gallery **6**
Warwick's **8**
Westfield UTC **9**

North County Shopping

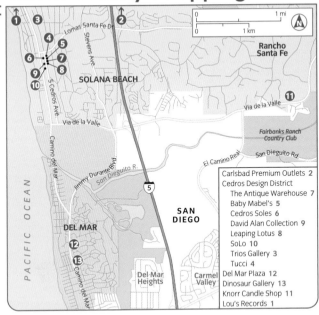

Carlsbad Premium Outlets 2
Cedros Design District
   The Antique Warehouse 7
   Baby Mabel's 5
   Cedros Soles 6
   David Alan Collection 9
   Leaping Lotus 8
   SoLo 10
   Trios Gallery 3
   Tucci 4
Del Mar Plaza 12
Dinosaur Gallery 13
Knorr Candle Shop 11
Lou's Records 1

Shopping **A to Z**

Antiques & Collectibles

★ **Antiques on Kettner** LITTLE ITALY Nearly 30 individual dealers share this space with a wide selection of quality antiques and collectibles. *2400 Kettner Blvd., Suite 106 (at W. Kalmia St.).* ☎ *619/234-3332. www.antiquesonkettner.com. MC, V. Bus: 83. Map p 71.*

★ **Ocean Beach Antiques District** OCEAN BEACH San Diego's greatest concentration of antiques stores are found along the main drag of Ocean Beach. There are several mall-style shops featuring dozens of dealers under one roof. *4800 block of Newport Ave. (at Sunset Cliffs Blvd.). www.antiquesinsandiego.com. AE, DISC, MC, V. Bus: 35 or 923. Map p 71.*

★★★ **Ruderman Antique Maps** LA JOLLA History buffs won't want to miss this place—it sells maps, atlases, and books that date from the 15th through 19th centuries. *7463 Girard Ave. (at Pearl St.).* ☎ *858/551-8500. www.rare maps.com. AE, DISC, MC, V. Bus: 30. Map p 73.*

Art

★★ **Africa and Beyond** LA JOLLA A collection of contemporary and traditional African sculpture, textiles, jewelry, and furnishings. *1250 Prospect St. (east of Ivanhoe Ave.).* ☎ *800/422-3742 or 858/454-9983. www.africaandbeyond.com. AE, DISC, MC, V. Bus: 30. Map p 73.*

★★ Chuck Jones Gallery

GASLAMP QUARTER Animation cels by the likes of Dr. Seuss and Chuck Jones, creator of Bugs Bunny and Daffy Duck, as well as classic Hollywood glamour photography. *232 Fifth Ave. (at K St.).* ☎ *619/294-9880. www.chuckjones.com. AE, DC, DISC, MC, V. Trolley: Gaslamp Quarter. Map p 71.*

★★★ Joseph Bellows Gallery

LA JOLLA Devotees of photography will want to check out this gallery, which showcases both contemporary and vintage work. *7661 Girard Ave. (btw. Kline St. and Torrey Pines Rd.).* ☎ *858/456-5620. www.josephbellows.com. AE, DISC, MC, V. Bus: 30. Map p 73.*

★★★ Quint Contemporary Art

LA JOLLA At press time this gallery was seeking a new permanent home in La Jolla. Its status as perhaps the city's finest contemporary art gallery makes it worth seeking out. ☎ *858/454-3409. www.quint gallery.com. AE, MC, V.*

★ Spanish Village Art Center

BALBOA PARK A collection of 37 casitas provide a home for some 250 artists working in everything from origami to glass. You can watch live as the artists do their thing. *1770 Village Pl. (in Balboa Park).* ☎ *619/233-9050. www.spanishvillageart.com. Most studios accept MC, V. Bus: 7. Map p 72.*

Chuck Jones art gallery.

★★ Tasende Gallery LA JOLLA

With its modern architecture and serene environs, this museum-like sculpture gallery provides a calm respite from the commercial hubbub nearby. *820 Prospect St. (at Jenner St.).* ☎ *858/454-3691. www.tasendegallery.com. No credit cards. Bus: 30. Map p 73.*

Books

★★ D.G. Wills Books LA JOLLA

This charmingly musty shop has books stacked to its wood rafters. If you're looking for something scholarly, offbeat, or esoteric, this is the place for you. *7461 Girard Ave. (at Pearl St.).* ☎ *858/456-1800. www.dgwillsbooks.com. AE, DISC, MC, V. Bus: 30. Map p 73.*

Shopping for artwork at Spanish Village Art Center.

Baby Mabel's maternity clothes.

★★★ **Warwick's** LA JOLLA This family-run business has been here since the 1930s. It's a browser's delight with more than 40,000 titles in stock; authors also come in for readings several times a week at this pet-friendly spot. *7812 Girard Ave. (btw. Wall and Silverado sts.).* ☎ *858/454-0347. www.warwicks. com. AE, DC, DISC, MC, V. Bus: 30. Map p 73.*

Children: Fashion & Toys
★ kids **Apple Box** EMBARCADERO You'll find everything from puzzles and pull toys to rocking horses and toy chests in this store which specializes in wooden toys. *Seaport Village, 837 W. Harbor Dr., Suite C (at Kettner Blvd.).* ☎ *800/676-7529. www.appleboxtoys.com. AE, DISC, MC, V. Trolley: Orange Line to Seaport Village. Map p 71.*

★★ **Baby Mabel's** SOLANA BEACH Hip fashions and gifts for infants and style-conscious moms-to-be. *136 S. Cedros Ave. (south of Lomas Santa Fe Dr.).* ☎ *858/794-0066. www.babymabels.com. AE, DISC, MC, V. Bus: 101. Coaster: Solana Beach. Map p 74.*

★★ kids **Quiksilver/Roxy** LA JOLLA Teens and 'tweens will love the surf and skate gear at this conjoined boys/girls shop in the heart of La Jolla village. *1111 Prospect St. (at*

Herschel Ave.). ☎ *858/459-1267. www.quiksilver.com. AE, DISC, MC, V. Bus: 30. Map p 73.*

Fashion
★★★ **Carol Gardyne** LITTLE ITALY You'll find one-of-a-kind and limited edition silk scarves and wall hangings, hand-painted at this studio/boutique. *1840 Columbia St. (at Fir St.).* ☎ *619/233-8066. www.carolgardyne. com. AE, DISC, MC, V. Bus: 83. Trolley: County Center/Little Italy. Map p 71.*

★★ **Cedros Soles** SOLANA BEACH Just try to resist the fabulous shoes for women here; there's also a great selection of handbags and other accessories. *143 S. Cedros Ave., Suite L (south of Lomas Santa Fe Dr.).* ☎ *858/794-9911. www.cedrossoles. com. AE, DISC, MC, V. Bus: 101. Coaster: Solana Beach. Map p 74.*

★★ **GOGA by Gordana** GASLAMP QUARTER Hip and glamorous women's fashion from Project Runway contestant Gordana Gehlhausen. *401 Market St. (at Fourth Ave.).* ☎ *619/564-7660. www.shop goga.com. AE, DISC, MC, V. Bus: 3, 11, or 120. Trolley: Convention Center. Map p 71.*

★★ **G-Star Raw** GASLAMP QUARTER This international chain has a cool San Diego boutique, selling

Surfer and skater gear at Quiksilver/Roxy in La Jolla.

What's trending at GOGA.

Euro-style denim. *470 Fifth Ave. (btw. Island Ave. and J St.).* ☎ *619/238-7088. www.g-star.com. AE, DISC, MC, V. Bus: 992. Trolley: Gaslamp Quarter. Map p 71.*

★★★ **Laura Gambucci** LA JOLLA Bucking the conservative La Jolla trend, this women's boutique features unique, contemporary styles and sexy shoes and handbags. *7629 Girard Ave., Suite C3 (btw. Kline St. and Torrey Pines Rd.).* ☎ *858/551-0214. AE, DISC, MC, V. Bus: 30. Map p 73.*

★★ **Mint** HILLCREST An excellent selection of urban sneakers and casual footwear for him and her. *525 University Ave. (btw. 5th and 6th aves.).* ☎ *619/291-6468. www.mintshoes.com. AE, MC, V. Bus: 1, 3, 10, 11, or 120. Map p 72.*

★★ **Sauvage** LA JOLLA Hit the sand in style with some fabulous beach- and swimwear from this local line. This sleek, chic boutique has a selection for the guys, too. *1025 Prospect St. (btw. Girard and Herschel aves.).* ☎ *858/729-0015. www.sauvagewear.com. AE, DC, DISC, MC, V. Bus: 30. Map p 73.*

★★ **Tucci** SOLANA BEACH This boutique is chic and sophisticated, offering contemporary, international designs in a comfortably mod space. *130 S. Cedros Ave., Ste. 140 (south of Lomas Santa Fe Dr.).* ☎ *858/259-8589. www.tucciboutique.com. AE, MC, V. Bus: 101. Coaster: Solana Beach. Map p 74.*

★★★ **Wear It Again Sam** HILLCREST This classy vintage clothing store sells high-quality goods from the 1920s through the '50s. *3823 Fifth Ave. (btw. University and Robinson aves.).* ☎ *619/299-0185. www.wearitagainsamvintage.com. AE, MC, V. Bus: 1, 3, 10, 11, or 120. Map p 72.*

Gifts

★ **Babette Schwartz** HILLCREST Camp meets kitsch at this fun-loving gift store stocked with novelties, cards, and T-shirts. *421 University Ave. (btw. 4th and 5th aves.).* ☎ *619/220-7048. www.babette.com. MC, V. Bus: 1, 3, 10, 11, or 120. Map p 72.*

★★ **kids Dinosaur Gallery** DEL MAR Own a piece of (pre)history—fossils, gems and minerals, and amber jewelry. Models, puzzles, and more for the kids, too. *1327 Camino Del Mar (btw. 13th and 14th sts.).* ☎ *858/794-4855. AE, MC, V. Bus: 101. Map p 74.*

★★ **Kita Ceramics & Glassware** GASLAMP QUARTER Objets d'art from Italy, Japan, and San Diego, including Murano glass jewelry and

Tucci in Solana Beach.

Boomerang for Modern in Little Italy.

lighting, pottery, and home accessories. *517 Fourth Ave., Ste. 101 (at Island Ave.). ☎ 619/239-2600. www.kitaceramicsglass.com. AE, MC, V. Bus: 992. Trolley: Convention Center. Map p 71.*

★★ **Knorr Candle Shop** DEL MAR This family-run business has been making beeswax candles here since 1928; it's one of the largest candle stores in the country. *14906 Via de la Valle (east of El Camino Real). ☎ 858/755-2051. www.knorrcandleshop.com. AE, DISC, MC, V. Bus: 308. Map p 74.*

Home Decor
★★★ **Cedros Design District** SOLANA BEACH   More than two-dozen chic and eclectic shops. Highlights include The Antique Warehouse (212 S. Cedros Ave.; ☎ 858/755-5156; DISC, MC, V); David Alan Collection (241 S. Cedros Ave.; ☎ 858/481-8044; www.thedavidalancollection.com; AE, DISC, MC, V); Leaping Lotus (240 S. Cedros Ave.; ☎ 858/720-8283; www.leapinglotus.com; AE, MC, V); SoLo, (309 S. Cedros Ave.; ☎ 858/794-9016; www.solocedros.com; AE, DISC, MC, V); and Trios Gallery (404 N. Cedros Ave.; ☎ 858/793-6040; www.triosgallery.com; AE, DISC, MC, V). *Primarily the 100 and 200 blocks of S. Cedros Ave. (south of Lomas Santa Fe Dr.). www.*

cedrosavenue.com. Bus: 101. Coaster: Solana Beach. Map p 74.

★★ **Column One** HILLCREST Classical and contemporary statuary and fountains for the home and garden. *401 University Ave., Ste. C. (at 4th Ave.). ☎ 619/299-9074. www.columnonesd.com. AE, DISC, MC, V. Bus: 1, 3, 10, 11, or 120. Map p 72.*

★★ **Emilia Castillo** LA JOLLA From her studio in Taxco, Mexico, Emilia Castillo produces fantastic, one-of-a-kind silver, gold, and porcelain home decor and jewelry. *1273 Prospect St. (east of Ivanhoe Ave.). ☎ 858/551-9600. www.emiliacastillolajolla.com. AE, DISC, MC, V. Bus: 30. Map p 73.*

★★ **Kettner Art & Design District** LITTLE ITALY   A conglomeration of cool stores and art galleries highlight this appealing neighborhood. Standouts include Mixture (2210 Kettner Blvd.; ☎ 619/239-4788; www.mixturedesigns.com; AE, MC, V); Boomerang for Modern (2475 Kettner Blvd.; ☎ 619/239-2040; www.boomerangformodern.com; AE, DISC, MC, V); and Scott White Contemporary Art (939 W. Kalmia St.; ☎ 619/501-5689; www.scottwhiteart.com; AE, MC, V). *Kettner Blvd. and India St. btw. Laurel and Date sts. Bus: 83. Trolley: County Center/Little Italy. Map p 71.*

★★★ **Mid-Century** HILLCREST Way-cool pottery, light fixtures, cocktail accessories, furniture, and more from the 1940s, '50s, and '60s. *3795 Park Blvd. ☎ 619/295-4832. AE, DISC, MC, V. Bus: 7. Map p 72.*

★★ **My Own Space** LA JOLLA Modern and minimalist furniture and accessories (with a touch of whimsy) highlight this sleek boutique. *7840 Girard Ave. (btw. Silverado and Wall sts.). ☎ 866/607-7223 or 858/459-0099. www.mosmyownspace.com. AE, V. Bus: 30. Map p 73.*

Jewelry

★★ Blondstone LA JOLLA
Creative jewelry designs, including unique rings, pendants, earrings, and bracelets incorporating sea-shells and tumbled sea-glass "mermaid tears." *925 Prospect St. (at Drury Lane).* ☎ *858/456-1994. www.blondstone.com. AE, MC, V. Bus: 30. Map p 73.*

★★★ Taboo Studio MISSION
HILLS The jewelry here is more than just simple ornamentation; these pieces are works of art created by nationally and internationally known jewelry artists. *1615½ W. Lewis St. (btw. Stephens St. and Palmetto Way).* ☎ *619/692-0099. www.taboostudio. com. AE, DISC, MC, V. Bus: 83. Map p 72.*

Music

★★★ Folk Arts Rare Records
NORMAL HEIGHTS Nirvana for serious collectors of jazz, folk, blues, and country music. A huge selection of 78s and other rarities; if you don't have a turntable, the store also can create custom recordings on CD. *2881 Adams Ave. (at Kansas St.).* ☎ *619/282-7833. www.folkarts rarerecords.com. MC, V. Bus: 11. Map p 72.*

★★★ Lou's Records ENCINITAS
A mind-blowing spot for anyone seriously into music or movies. A compound of buildings dedicated to new and imported CDs, used CDs and vinyl, as well as DVDs. *434 N. Coast Hwy. 101 (btw. El Portal St. and North Court).* ☎ *888/568-7732 or 760/753-1382. www.lousrecords.com. AE, DISC, MC, V. Bus: 101. Map p 74.*

Shopping Centers

★★★ Carlsbad Premium Outlets CARLSBAD
Some of the biggest names in fashion and retail are elbow to elbow at this smart and handsome outlet mall featuring some 90 stores. It has a fine-dining component, too. *5600 Paseo del Norte (adjacent to I-5).* ☎ *888/790-7467 or 760/804-9000. www.premiumoutlets. com. Bus: 321. Map p 74.*

★★★ Del Mar Plaza DEL MAR
With its oceanview terraces, fountains, destination restaurants, and open-air wine bar, this might be the nicest mall you've ever seen. There are more than 30 shops and eateries. *1555 Camino Del Mar (at 15th St.).* ☎ *858/792-1555. www.delmar plaza.com. Bus: 101. Map p 74.*

★★ Fashion Valley Center MIS-
SION VALLEY This upscale shopping center features Nordstrom and Neiman Marcus department stores, as well as more than 200 specialty shops and an 18-screen movie theater. *7007 Friars Rd. (btw. Hwy. 163 and Fashion Valley Rd.).* ☎ *619/688-9113. www.simon.com. Bus: 6, 14, 20, 25, 41, 120, or 928. Trolley: Blue or Green Line to Fashion Valley. Map p 72.*

★★ Horton Plaza GASLAMP
QUARTER This colorful shopping center has more than 130 specialty shops, a performing arts venue, a

My Own Space in La Jolla.

POP ♦ JAZZ VOCALS・H...

GoGI GRANT
EARL GRANT
ROBERT GOULET

GEORGIA GIB

Folk Arts Rare Records.

14-screen cinema, two major department stores, and a variety of restaurants and short-order eateries. *324 Horton Plaza (bounded by Broadway, 1st and 4th aves., and G St.).* ☎ *619/ 239-8180. www.westfield.com/ hortonplaza. Bus: 2, 3, 5, 7, 11, 15, 20, 30, 50, 120, 150, 210, 850, 860, 901, 923, 929, or 992. Trolley: Blue or Orange Line to Civic Center. Map p 71.*

Seaport Village outdoor mall.

Mission Valley Center MISSION VALLEY   This old-fashioned outdoor mall has budget-minded offerings like Nordstrom Rack outlet store and Target, plus a 20-screen movie theater and 150 other stores and places to eat. *1640 Camino del Rio N. (alongside I-8 at Mission Center Rd.).* ☎ *619/296-6375. www. westfield.com/missionvalley. Bus: 6 or 14. Trolley: Blue or Green Line to Mission Valley Center. Map p 72.*

★ **kids Seaport Village** EMBARCADERO   This 14-acre (5.5-hectare) bayfront outdoor mall provides an idyllic setting that visitors love. Many of the more than 50 shops are of the Southern California cutesy variety, but the atmosphere is pleasant, and there are a few gems. *849 W. Harbor Dr. (at Kettner Blvd.).* ☎ *619/235-4014. www.seaport village.com. Trolley: Orange Line to Seaport Village. Map p 71.*

★ **Westfield UTC** LA JOLLA   This outdoor shopping complex has a shady, landscaped plaza and more than 150 stores, including Nordstrom and Macy's. It's also home to a year-round ice-skating rink. *4545 La Jolla Village Dr. (at Genesee Ave.).* ☎ *858/ 546-8858. www.westfield.com/utc. Bus: 30, 31, 50, 101, 105, 150, 201, 202, 880, or 960. Map p 73.* ●

The Best **Beaches**

Black's Beach 7
Burger Lounge 12
Children's Pool 10
Coronado Beach 17
Del Mar Beach 5
Imperial Beach 18
La Jolla Cove 9
La Jolla Shores 8
Mission Bay Park 15
Mission Beach 14
North County Beaches
  Boneyards Beach 3
  Moonlight Beach 2
  Oceanside 1
  Swami's Beach 4
Ocean Beach 16
Pacific Beach 13
Torrey Pines Beach 6
Windansea Beach 11

Previous page: A game of volleyball at Del Mar Beach.

San Diego County is blessed with **70 miles (113km) of sandy coastline** and more than 30 individual beaches. Even in winter and spring, when water temperatures drop into the 50s, the beaches are great places to walk, jog, and surf. In summer, when the beaches teem with locals and visitors alike, the bikinis come out, pecs are flexed, and a spring-break atmosphere threatens to break loose.

★★★ **Black's Beach.** Located at the base of steep, 300-foot-high (91m) cliffs, this 2-mile-long (3km) beach is out of the way and not easy to reach, but it draws scores with its secluded beauty and good swimming and surfing conditions—the graceful spectacle of paragliders launching from the cliffs above adds to the show. This is the area's unofficial nude beach, though technically nude sunbathing is illegal. Citations are rarely issued—lifeguards will either ignore it or just ask you to cover up. (Tickets will be written if you disregard their request.) There are no facilities here. *Bus: 101 to the Torrey Pines Gliderport; hike down the trail. You can also walk to Black's from beaches south (La Jolla Shores) or north (Torrey Pines).*

The 🍵 ★ **Burger Lounge** is a fast-food joint—La Jolla-style. This sleek and modern burger spot has plenty of panache—it's casual but fashionable, serving grass-fed, organic beef burgers, as well as hand-cut fries and salads. Milkshakes, wine, and beer are also on the short menu. *1101 Wall St. (at Herschel Ave.).* ☎ *858/456-0196. www.burger lounge.com. Sun–Thurs 10:30am–9pm, Fri–Sat 10:30am–10pm. $8.*

Sea lions loll on the beach at the Children's Pool.

★★ kids **Children's Pool.** Think clothing-optional Black's Beach is the city's most controversial sun-sea-sand situation? Think again—the Children's Pool is currently home to the biggest man-vs.-beast struggle since *Moby Dick*. A sea wall shields this pocket of sand, originally intended as a calm swimming bay for children, but since 1994, when an offshore rock outcrop was designated as a protected mammal reserve, the beach has been cordoned off for the resident harbor seal population. The water can be foul, but swimming has been re-instated here—under the watchful eye of seal-loving volunteers—but most people just come to observe the colony. *See p 60, bullet ❸. Bus: 30 to Girard Ave. and Silverado St. Walk 2 blocks down Girard Ave., cross Prospect St. to Ocean Lane.*

★★★ kids **Coronado Beach.** Lovely, wide, and sparkling, this beach is conducive to strolling and lingering, especially in the late afternoon. At the north end, you can watch fighter jets flying in formation from the Naval base, while just south is the pretty section fronting Ocean Boulevard and the Hotel del Coronado. Waves are gentle here, so the beach draws many Coronado families—and their dogs, which are allowed off-leash at the most north-westerly end. South of the Hotel Del, the beach becomes the beautiful, often deserted Silver Strand. The islands visible from here, Los Coronados, are 18 miles away and belong to Mexico. *Bus: 901 or 904 to the Hotel Del Coronado.*

★★ kids **Del Mar Beach.** The Del Mar Thoroughbred Club's slogan, as famously sung by DMTC founder Bing Crosby, is "where turf meets the surf." This town beach represents the "surf" portion of that phrase. It's a long stretch of sand backed by grassy cliffs and a playground area; several restaurants offer dining right alongside the beach. Del Mar is about 15 miles (24km) from downtown San Diego. *Bus: 101.*

★ **Imperial Beach.** A half-hour south of downtown San Diego by car or trolley, and only a few minutes from the Mexican border, Imperial Beach is popular with surfers and local youth, who can be somewhat territorial about "their" beach in summer. I.B., as it's known, has 3 miles (5km) of surf breaks plus a guarded "swimmers only" stretch; check with lifeguards before getting wet, though, since sewage runoff from nearby Mexico can sometimes foul the water. I.B. also plays host to the annual U.S. Open Sandcastle Competition in late July—the best reason to come here—with world-class sand creations ranging from nautical scenes to dinosaurs. *Trolley: Blue Line to Palm Ave., transfer to Bus 933/934.*

Del Mar Beach.

★★★ **kids** **La Jolla Cove.** The star of postcards for more than a century, the tropical-hued waters of La Jolla Cove represent San Diego at its most picture-perfect. Part of the San Diego–La Jolla Underwater Ecological Reserve, the Cove is a perfect place to do some snorkeling or kayaking. If the small beach gets a little too crowded, classy, grassy Ellen Browning Scripps Park on the bluff above it provides a great alternative. *See p 60, bullets* ④ *and* ⑤. *Bus: 30. Walking directions same as previous.*

★★ **kids** **La Jolla Shores.** The wide, flat mile of sand at La Jolla Shores is popular with joggers, swimmers, kayakers, novice scuba divers, and beginning body- and board-surfers, as well as families. Weekend crowds can be enormous, quickly claiming fire rings and occupying both the sand and the metered parking spaces in the lot. There are restrooms, showers, and picnic areas here, as well as palm-lined Kellogg Park across the street.

Bus: 30 to La Jolla Shores Dr. and Avenida de la Playa. Walk 5 blocks down Avenida de la Playa.

★ **kids** **Mission Bay Park.** This 4,600-acre (1,862-hectare) aquatic playground contains 27 miles (43km) of bayfront, picnic areas and children's playgrounds, and paths for biking, in-line skating, and jogging. The bay lends itself to windsurfing, sailing, water-skiing, and fishing. There are dozens of access points; one of the most popular is off I-5 at Clairemont Drive. Also accessed from this spot is Fiesta Island, where the annual softball-cum-beach party spectacle known as the Over the Line Tournament is held to raucous enthusiasm in July; a 4-mile (6.5km) road loops around the island. Vacation Island, in the center of the bay, is home to Paradise Point Resort (see p 142) and Ski Beach. Parts of the bay have been subject to closure over the years due to high levels of bacteria, so check for posted warnings. Personally, I'd rather sail on Mission Bay than swim in it. *Bus: 8/9 or 30. See p 92.*

Half-mile long, sandy Del Mar Beach.

The pier at Imperial Beach.

★ **Mission Beach.** While Mission Bay Park is a body of salt water surrounded by land and bridges, Mission Beach is actually a beach on the Pacific Ocean, anchored by the Giant Dipper roller coaster and the Belmont Park amusement center. Always popular, the sands and wide cement boardwalk sizzle with activity and great people-watching in summer; at the southern end a volleyball game is almost always underway. The long beach and path extend from the jetty north to Belmont Park and Pacific Beach Drive. Parking is often tough, with your best bets being the public lots at Belmont Park or at the south end of West Mission Bay Drive. Busy Mission Boulevard is the centerline of a 2-block-wide isthmus that separates the ocean and Mission Bay; it stretches a mile north to Pacific Beach. *Bus: 8/9 to Mission Beach.*

North County Beaches. Those inclined to venture farther north in San Diego County won't be disappointed. Pacific Coast Highway leads to inviting beaches, such as these in Encinitas: peaceful ★★ **Boneyard Beach**, ★★★ **Swami's Beach** for surfing, and ★★ **Moonlight Beach,** popular with families and

Sunset at Pacific Beach.

volleyball buffs. Farthest north is ★★ **Oceanside,** which has one of the West Coast's longest wooden piers, wide sandy beaches, and several popular surfing areas. *Bus: 101. Coaster: Encinitas or Oceanside.*

★ **Ocean Beach.** Officially known as Dog Beach, the northern end of Ocean Beach Park is one of only a few in the county where your pooch can roam freely on the sand and frolic with several dozen other people's pets. Surfers generally congregate around the O.B. Pier, mostly in the water but often at the snack shack on the end. Rip currents can be strong here and sometimes discourage swimmers from venturing beyond waist depth (check with the lifeguard stations). Facilities at the beach include restrooms, showers, picnic tables, volleyball courts, and plenty of metered parking lots. *Bus: 35 or 923 to Newport Ave.*

★ **Pacific Beach.** There's always action here, particularly along Ocean Front Walk, a paved promenade featuring a human parade akin to that at L.A.'s Venice Beach boardwalk. It runs along Ocean Boulevard (just west of Mission Blvd.) to the pier. Surfing is popular year-round here, in marked sections, and the beach is well staffed with lifeguards. You're on your own to find street parking. Pacific Beach is also the home of Tourmaline Surfing Park, a half-mile (.8km) north of the pier, where the sport's old guard gathers to surf waters where swimmers are prohibited; reach it via Tourmaline Street, off Mission Boulevard. *Bus: 8/9.*

★★★ **Torrey Pines Beach.** At the foot of Torrey Pines State Reserve is this fabulous, underused strand, accessed by a pay parking lot at the entrance to the park. In fact, combining a visit to the park

Hang gliding at Torrey Pines

with a day at the beach makes for the quintessential San Diego outdoor experience. It's rarely crowded, though you need to be aware of high tide (when most of the sand gets a bath). In almost any weather, it's a great beach for walking. ***Warning:*** At this and any other bluff-side beach, never sit at the bottom of the cliffs. The hillsides are unstable and could collapse. *Bus: 101.*

★★ **Windansea Beach.** The fabled locale of Tom Wolfe's *Pump House Gang,* Windansea is legendary to this day among California's surf elite and remains one of San Diego's prettiest strands. This is not a good beach for swimming or diving, so come to surf (no novices, please), watch surfers, or soak in the camaraderie and party atmosphere. Windansea has no facilities, and street parking is first-come, first-served. *Bus: 30 to Nautilus St.*

Cabrillo National Monument

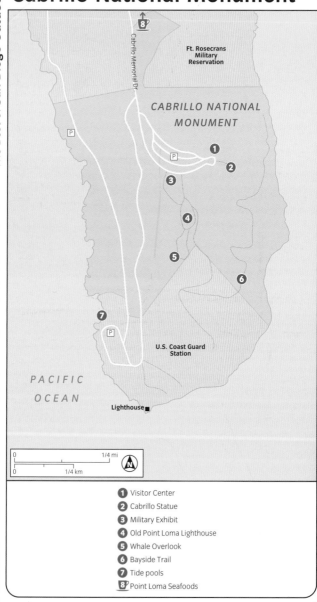

Cabrillo Memorial Dr.

Ft. Rosecrans
Military
Reservation

CABRILLO NATIONAL
MONUMENT

P

P

U.S. Coast Guard
Station

PACIFIC
OCEAN

Lighthouse ■

0   1/4 mi
0   1/4 km

1 Visitor Center
2 Cabrillo Statue
3 Military Exhibit
4 Old Point Loma Lighthouse
5 Whale Overlook
6 Bayside Trail
7 Tide pools
8 Point Loma Seafoods

On this day, Thursday, September 28, 1542, we discovered a port, closed and very good."** When Juan Rodríguez Cabrillo led his three galleons into that sheltered harbor some 470 years ago, he became the first European to set eyes on what would become the West Coast of the United States. Point Loma, the spit of land that protected Cabrillo and his flotilla from an oncoming storm, is now the site of Cabrillo National Monument, a 160-acre (65-hectare) national park that is rich not only in history, but in natural wonders as well. START: **Bus route 84.**

① ★★ **Visitor Center.** Start your tour here. The visitor center has a bookstore with numerous publications on San Diego history, marine life, and the age of exploration in the 16th century. There's also a glassed-in observation area offering stellar panoramas, including views of the actual spot where Cabrillo's party came ashore. The park's auditorium has ongoing screenings of films about Cabrillo's journey, whale migration, and more; a small museum features interactive exhibits about the conquistador and Spain's far-flung empire. Declared a National Monument in 1913 by President Woodrow Wilson, the park is also the site of special events, including a reenactment of Cabrillo's landing every late

The new Point Loma Lighthouse.

Cabrillo overlooking the landscape he discovered for Spain in 1542.

September/early October, and whale-related festivities every winter. *See p 13, bullet* **①**.

② ★★ **Cabrillo Statue.** This 15-foot (4.5m) statue portrays Cabrillo looking steadfast and resolute; he doesn't seem to be much enjoying the 360-degree view from his privileged position. The flesh-and-blood Cabrillo was Portuguese (actual name, João Rodrigues Cabrilho), and as a soldier serving Spain he made a name for himself as a crossbowman during Hernán Cortés's siege of Tenochtitlán (now Mexico City), and also participated in the conquest of Guatemala. His adventuring would come to an end several months after his visit to San Diego when he died from an injury suffered in a skirmish with Chumash Indians on one of Southern California's Channel Islands.

③ **Military Exhibit.** Point Loma's strategic importance has long been recognized, and the area was established as a military reserve in 1852. Long-range gun batteries bristled from this plateau during both world wars, and their remnants are still here. In a small building once used as an army radio station, there is an exhibit documenting San Diego's 19th Coast Artillery and the war hysteria that gripped the city after the attack on Pearl Harbor.

The Point Loma lighthouse.

operation since 1891. An interactive exhibit details what life was like for the keepers who lived here in the 19th century, far from the relative comforts of Old Town; the lighthouse itself is filled with period furnishings.

5 ★ **Whale Overlook.** From this sheltered space, you can spot Pacific gray whales as they make their amazing, 10,000-mile (16,093km) journey from the Bering Sea to the warm lagoons of Mexico's Sea of Cortés, and back again, every mid-December through mid-March. These 40-ton (36T), 50-foot (15m) behemoths (with calves in tow on the return trip) are making the longest migration of any mammal. The overlook is outfitted with recorded information and high-powered telescopes; if you don't manage to see a whale, you can still have your picture taken with the scaled-down whale sculpture nearby.

4 ★★ **Old Point Loma Light-house.** This lighthouse had a relatively short lifespan (1855–91), its seemingly perfect location compromised by low clouds and fog that often rendered the sweeping beam of light useless. The New Point Loma Lighthouse, situated nearby at sea level, has been in continuous

6 ★★★ **Bayside Trail.** This trail meanders through a coastal sage ecosystem that has all but disappeared from Southern California. The hiking is easy—the trail is only 2.5 miles (4km) round-trip—but the bay views are spectacular, and there are

Trail between the lighthouse and the Whale Overlook.

Federally protected tide pools at Cabrillo National Monument.

informative signs posted along the way, identifying and explaining the local flora and fauna. Audio stations providing historical details in six different languages are located at various sites throughout the park, as well, and rangers and docents often present a variety of talks and guided walks.

7 ★★★ kids Tide Pools.
Cabrillo National Monument has the only federally protected tide pools on the Southern California mainland. This rocky, intertidal ecosystem hosts a variety of sea life, including crabs, starfish, octopi, and anemones. For the best tide pooling, call ahead to find out when low tide is happening; otherwise, there may not be much to see—other than the awe-inspiring cliffs and ocean vistas. ☎ 619/557-5450. **Note:** *Exercise caution when exploring tide pools, the rocks are slippery; do not handle the animals; expect to get a little bit wet.*

There are no food facilities at Cabrillo National Monument so consider stopping by the deli-style seafood market

8 ★★ Point Loma Seafoods
before or after visiting the park. This San Diego institution is usually chaos, especially around lunchtime, but this is the place for fresh-off-the-boat fish. *2805 Emerson St. (at Scott St.).* ☎ *619/223-1109. www.pointloma seafoods.com. Mon–Thurs 9am–6:30pm, Fri–Sat 9am–7pm, Sun 10am–7pm. $8–$16.*

Rough surf at Cabrillo National Monument.

Mission Bay Park

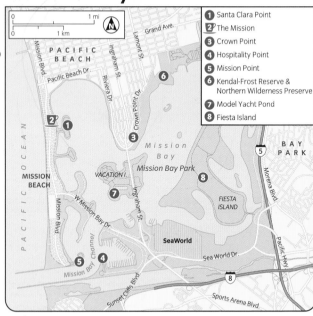

1 Santa Clara Point
2 The Mission
3 Crown Point
4 Hospitality Point
5 Mission Point
6 Kendal-Frost Reserve & Northern Wilderness Preserve
7 Model Yacht Pond
8 Fiesta Island

Originally known as False Bay, this swampy marshland was transformed in the 1940s into Mission Bay Park. This vast outdoor playground encompasses more than 4,200 acres (1,700 hectares)—about half of it water, half of it land—with 27 miles (43km) of shoreline, 19 sandy beaches, grassy parks, wildlife preserves, boat docks and launches (with rental facilities), basketball courts, and an extensive system of pathways. Locals and visitors alike flock to Mission Bay for everything from kite flying to powerboating.

START: **Bus 8/9 to Santa Clara Pl.**

1 ★★ kids **Santa Clara Point.** Recreation centers don't get any cooler than the city-run facility here. Surrounded by the bay waters, it features tennis courts, a softball field, lighted basketball courts, a playground, and weight room. Also on the point is Mission Bay Sport-center, where you can rent sailboats, catamarans, pedal boats, sailboards, kayaks, WaveRunners,

motorboats, or surfboards. *Recreation Center, 1008 Santa Clara Place.* ☎ *858/581-9928. www.sandiego. gov. Mon, Wed, Fri noon–7pm, Tues & Thurs noon–7:30pm, Sat 10am–2pm, closed Sun. Mission Bay Sport-center, 1010 Santa Clara Place.* ☎ *858/488-1004; www.mission baysportcenter.com. Daily 9am–7pm. Bus: 8/9.*

Palms in Mission Bay Park.

too—it builds a floating nest among the stands of cordgrass.

7 ★ kids Model Yacht Pond. Sailboats and powerboats are ubiquitous features on Mission Bay, but many people are unaware of the flotilla that plies the waters of the Model Yacht Pond in the middle of Vacation Island. Just about any weekend you can find hobbyists with their sophisticated, radio-controlled crafts competing or just having fun. Some of these models are amazingly detailed replicas of historic ships like Spanish galleons or World War II battleships; others are ferocious little hydroplanes capable of speeds in excess of 60 mph (97kmph). *Bus: 8/9 to W. Vacation Rd.*

8 Fiesta Island. If you've got Fido in tow, this is a great place to let him run leash-free to his heart's content. This is the largest individual piece of Mission Bay Park, a rather barren island at the eastern edge of the bay, often used for events like the Over-the-Line

softball tournament in July and cycling time trials and races. There is a 4-mile (6.5km) road that loops around the island, and fire rings are situated throughout. *Picnics are not permitted; there are no restrooms. Daily 6am–10pm. Bus: 105 to Sea-World Dr.*

Catamarans in De Anza Cove.

The Best **Hiking**

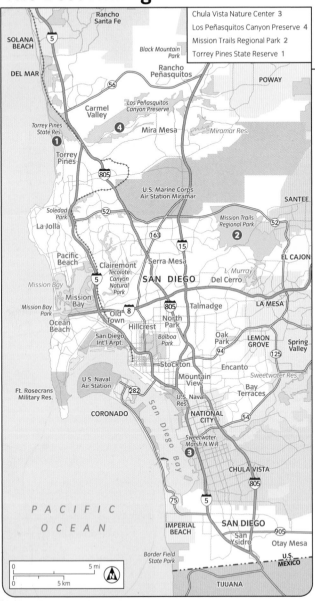

Chula Vista Nature Center 3
Los Peñasquitos Canyon Preserve 4
Mission Trails Regional Park 2
Torrey Pines State Reserve 1

Even from downtown, you don't have to venture far to discover San Diego's wild side. Whether you're looking for solitude along an oak-shaded trail or want to spot an endangered species in its natural habitat, you'll find nearby open-space preserves and parks that will satisfy any outdoor enthusiast. START: **Bus 101 to Torrey Pines State Reserve.**

1 ★★★ **Torrey Pines State Reserve.** One of San Diego's most treasured spots, this reserve is home to the country's rarest pine, the Torrey pine, which grows only here and on an island off the coast of Santa Barbara. The 1,750-acre (708-hectare) reserve was established in 1921, from a gift by Ellen Browning Scripps, and encompasses dramatic 300-foot-high (91m), water-carved sandstone bluffs, the beach below them, and a lagoon immediately north. Of the six different trails, none is longer than 1.5 miles (2km), and the aptly named Beach Trail provides access to the ocean; pick up a trail map at the small visitor center, built in the traditional adobe style of the Hopi Indians. Interpretive nature walks are held weekends and holidays at 10am and 2pm. *Hwy. 101 (btw. La Jolla and Del Mar).* ☎ *858/755-2063. www.torreypine. org. There are no facilities for food or drinks inside the park; you can bring a picnic lunch, but you have to eat it on the beach—food and drink (other than water) are not allowed in the upper portion of the reserve. Admission $10 per car ($9 for seniors). Daily 8am–sunset. Bus: 101.*

2 ★★ **Mission Trails Regional Park.** This is one of the nation's largest urban parks, a 5,800-acre (2,347-hectare) spread that includes abundant bird life, two lakes, a picturesque stretch of the San Diego River, the remains of the Old Mission Dam (probably the first irrigation project in the West), and 1,592-foot (485m) Cowles Mountain, the summit of which reveals outstanding views over much of the county. There are trails up to 4 miles (6.5km) in length—including a 1.5-mile (2.5km) interpretive trail—some of which are designated for mountain bike use. *1 Father Junipero Serra Trail.* ☎ *619/ 668-3275 or 619/668-3281. www. mtrp.org. Free admission. Daily sunrise to sundown (visitor center 9am– 5pm). Bus: 115 to Jackson Dr. and Navajo Rd., then 1.4 miles (2.25km) to the West Gate.*

3 ★★ **kids** **Chula Vista Nature Center.** This interpretive center set in the Sweetwater Marsh National Wildlife Refuge is just a 15-minute drive from downtown San Diego. There is a 1.5-mile (2.5km) loop trail through coastal wetlands where more than 220 different species of birds have been identified. The trail also features a photo blind and posted information on the flora and fauna. *See p 32, bullet* **10**.

4 ★★ **Los Peñasquitos Canyon Preserve.** Stretching for nearly 7 miles (11km), this 4,000-acre (1,619-hectare) preserve is an oasis amid the suburbia that surrounds it.

Hikers in Los Peñasquitos Canyon Preserve.

Farther Afield

Those in search of a wilderness experience will find ample room to roam in 650,000-acre (263,045-hectare) ★★★ Anza-Borrego Desert State Park, California's largest state park, or 26,000-acre (10,522-hectare) ★★ Cuyamaca Rancho State Park. Both are less than a 2-hour drive away from downtown San Diego.

The terrain at Anza-Borrego incorporates dry lake beds, sandstone canyons, granite mountains, palm groves fed by year-round springs, and more than 600 kinds of desert plants. The best time to come is in spring, when wildflowers burst into bloom, transforming the desert into a brilliant palette of pink, lavender, red, orange, and yellow. Your first stop here should be the architecturally striking Visitor Center (☎ 760/767-4205 or 760/767-5311; www.parks.ca.

Anza-Borrego Desert State Park.

gov)—in addition to a small museum, it offers information, maps, and audiovisual presentations; an interpreted loop trail is also on-site. The visitor center is open October through May, Thursday through Monday, from 9am to 5pm; June through September, weekends and holidays only, from 9am to 5pm.

Cuyamaca Rancho State Park is about 15 miles (24km) south of the historic mountain town of Julian (see p 150). Though badly burned in an epic firestorm in 2003, Mother Nature has recovered nicely in Cuyamaca. The most popular hikes are to 5,700-foot (1,737m) Stonewall Peak (2 miles/3km) and 6,500-foot (1,981m) Cuyamaca Peak (3.5 miles/5.5km)—both offer spectacular vistas. Trail heads for each are at Paso Picacho campground. Five miles (8km) south of that campground is Green Valley campground, where you'll find cool natural pools in which to splash (day use of campgrounds is $8 per vehicle; overnight is $30). The park is reached via Highway 79, 5 miles (8km) north of Interstate 8. For more information call ☎ 760/765-3020 or 760/765-0755, or go to www.cuyamaca.us.

The area was part of the first Mexican land grant in San Diego, and the historic Santa Maria de los Peñasquitos adobe ranch home (1823) still stands at the east end of the park (tours are Sat at 11am and Sun at 1pm). Along the trail are beautiful stands of oak and sycamore; there's also a waterfall that flows year-round. *12020 Black Mountain Rd.* ☎ *858/484-7504. www.sandiego. gov/park-and-recreation. Free admission. Daily 8am–sunset. Bus: 210 to Mira Mesa Blvd. and Black Mountain Rd., 1.3 miles (2km) farther north on Black Mountain Rd.* ●

Dining **Best Bets**

Best **Business Lunch**
★ Dobson's Bar & Restaurant $$–$$$ *956 Broadway Circle (p 108)*

Best **Mexican Food**
★★★ El Agave Tequileria $$–$$$ *2304 San Diego Ave. (p 108)*; and ★★★ Candelas $$$ *416 Third Ave. and 1201 First St. (p 107)*

Best **Breakfast with a View**
★ Brockton Villa $–$$ *1235 Coast Blvd. (p 106)*

Best **Lunch with a View**
★★★ Bertrand at Mister A's $$$$ *2550 Fifth Ave. (p 105)*

Best **Dinner with a View**
★★★ Georges California Modern $$$$ *1250 Prospect St. (p 109)*

Best **Use of Local Product (Sea)**
★★ Zenbu $$–$$$ *7660 Fay Ave. (p 112)*

Best **Use of Local Product (Land)**
★★ The Linkery $$ *3794 30th St. (p 110)*

Best **California Cuisine**
★★★ Blanca $$$$ *437 S. Coast Hwy. 101 (p 105)*

Best **Modern American Cuisine**
★★★ Market Restaurant + Bar $$$ *3702 Via de la Valle (p 110)*

Best **Steak**
★★ Cowboy Star $$–$$$$ *650 10th Ave. (p 107)*

Best **Pan-Asian Cuisine**
★★ Red Pearl Kitchen $$–$$$ *440 J St. (p 111)*

Best **Pizza**
★★ Bronx Pizza $–$$ *111 Washington St. (p 106)*

Best **Desserts**
★★★ Extraordinary Desserts $ *2929 Fifth Ave. and 1430 Union St. (p 108)*

Best **Bistro**
★★ Cafe Chloe $$–$$$ *721 Ninth Ave. (p 106)*

Best **Picnic Fare**
★★ Bread & Cie $ *350 University Ave. (p 106)*

Most **Romantic Dining Room**
★★★ The Marine Room $$$$ *2000 Spindrift Dr. (p 110)*

Best **Sushi**
★★★ Sushi Ota $$ *4529 Mission Bay Dr. (p 111)*

Best **Place for Hipster Foodies**
★★★ Cucina Urbana $$ *505 Laurel St. (p 108)*

Best **Late-Night Dining**
Brian's 24 Restaurant Bar & Grill $$ 828 Sixth Ave. (p 106)

Previous page: Café Pacifica.

Downtown Dining

Bertrand at Mister A's 2
Brian's 24 9
Cafe Chloe 10
Candelas 12
Cowboy Star 11
Cucina Urbana 3
Dobson's Bar & Restaurant 8
El Camino 4
Extraordinary Desserts 1, 6
Filippi's Pizza Grotto 5
The Fish Market / Top of
  the Market 7
Nobu 15
The Oceanaire Seafood Room 13
Red Pearl Kitchen 14

Hillcrest & Old Town Dining

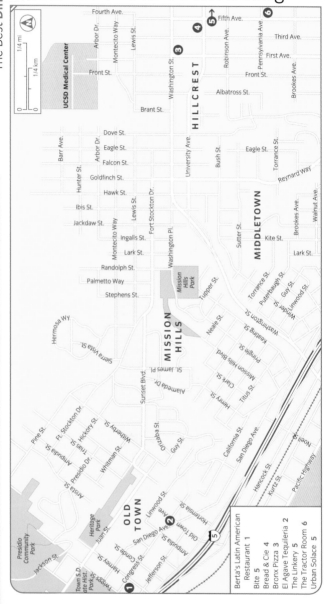

Berta's Latin American
  Restaurant 1
Bite 5
Bread & Cie 4
Bronx Pizza 3
El Agave Tequileria 2
The Linkery 5
The Tractor Room 6
Urban Solace 5

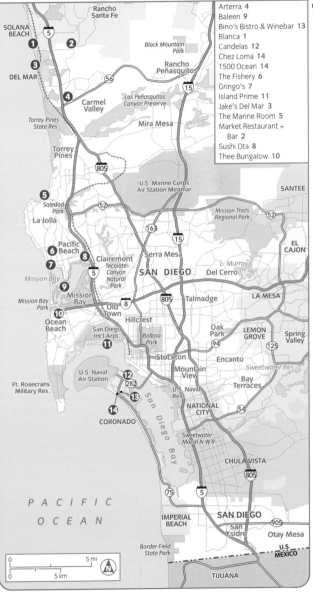

Beach Dining

SOLANA BEACH

Rancho Santa Fe

Black Mountain Park

DEL MAR

Rancho Peñasquitos

Carmel Valley

Los Peñasquitos Canyon Preserve

Mira Mesa

Torrey Pines State Res.

Torrey Pines

U.S. Marine Corps Air Station Miramar

SANTEE

Soledad Park

Mission Trails Regional Park

La Jolla

EL CAJON

Pacific Beach

Clairemont Tecolote Canyon Natural Park

Serra Mesa

SAN DIEGO

L. Murray Del Cerro

Mission Bay

LA MESA

Mission Bay Park

Mission Bay

Old Town

Talmadge

Ocean Beach

Hillcrest

San Diego Int'l Arpt.

Balboa Park

Oak Park

LEMON GROVE

Spring Valley

Stockton

Mountain View

Encanto

Sweetwater Res.

Ft. Rosecrans Military Res.

U.S. Naval Air Station

U.S. Naval Res.

Bay Terraces

NATIONAL CITY

CORONADO

San Diego Bay

Sweetwater Marsh N.W.R.

CHULA VISTA

PACIFIC OCEAN

IMPERIAL BEACH

SAN DIEGO

San Ysidro

Otay Mesa

Border Field State Park

U.S. MEXICO

TIJUANA

0   5 mi
0   5 km

Arterra **4**
Baleen **9**
Bino's Bistro & Winebar **13**
Blanca **1**
Candelas **12**
Chez Loma **14**
1500 Ocean **14**
The Fishery **6**
Gringo's **7**
Island Prime **11**
Jake's Del Mar **3**
The Marine Room **5**
Market Restaurant +
    Bar **2**
Sushi Ota **8**
Thee Bungalow **10**

La Jolla Dining

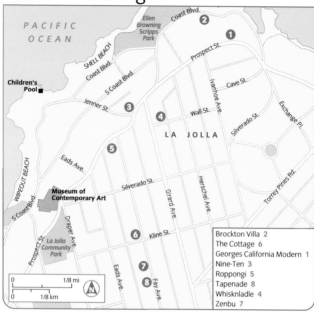

PACIFIC
OCEAN

Ellen Browning Scripps Park

Coast Blvd.

Prospect St.

SHELL BEACH

Coast Blvd.

S Coast Blvd.

Children's Pool

Jenner St.

Ivanhoe Ave.

Cave St.

Wall St.

LA JOLLA

Silverado St.

Exchange Pl.

Eads Ave.

WIPEOUT BEACH

S Coast Blvd.

Prospect St.

Museum of Contemporary Art

Silverado St.

Girard Ave.

Herschel Ave.

Torrey Pines Rd.

Draper Ave.

La Jolla Community Park

Kline St.

Eads Ave.

Fay Ave.

0   1/8 mi
0   1/8 km

Brockton Villa 2
The Cottage 6
Georges California Modern 1
Nine-Ten 3
Roppongi 5
Tapenade 8
Whisknladle 4
Zenbu 7

Dining **A to Z**

★★ 1500 Ocean CORONADO *CALIFORNIAN* The Hotel del Coronado's fine-dining option has a smart California Craftsman look and a Southland coastal cuisine menu that draws inspiration and top-quality products from throughout the region, from Baja to Santa Barbara. *1500 Orange Ave. (at the Hotel del Coronado).* ☎ *619/522-8490. www.dine1500ocean.com. Entrees $28–$46. AE, DC, DISC, MC, V. Tues–Thurs 5:30–9pm; Fri–Sat 5:30–10pm; bar Tues–Sat 5pm–midnight. Bus: 901 or 904.*

★★ Arterra DEL MAR *CALIFORNIAN* There's a stylish outdoor lounge and a menu that's regularly adapted to meet the schedule of Mother Earth,

featuring top products from local farms. *11966 El Camino Real (next to I-5 in the Marriott Del Mar).* ☎ *858/369-6032. www.arterrarestaurant. com. Entrees $7–$12 breakfast, $13–$32 lunch and dinner. AE, DC, DISC, MC, V. Breakfast Mon–Fri 6:30–10:30am, Sat–Sun 7–11am; lunch Mon–Fri 11:30am–2pm; dinner Tues–Thurs 5:30–9:30pm; lounge daily 11:30am–midnight (from 11am weekends).*

★★ kids Baleen MISSION BAY *SEAFOOD/CALIFORNIAN* This attractive, family-friendly waterfront eatery is right in the middle of Mission Bay—the perfect place to savor a selection of wood-roasted seafood. *1404 Vacation Rd. (Paradise*

Point Resort). ☎ 858/490-6363. www.paradisepoint.com. Entrees $22–$78. AE, DC, DISC, MC, V. Sun–Thurs 5–9pm; Fri–Sat 5–10pm. Bus: 8/9.

★ **Berta's Latin American Restaurant** OLD TOWN *LATIN AMERICAN* Faithfully re-creating the flavors of Central and South America, Berta's provides welcome relief from the nacho-and-fajita places that dominate Old Town. *3928 Twiggs St. (at Congress St.).* ☎ 619/295-2343. www.bertasin oldtown.com. Entrees $7–$12 lunch, $13–$17 dinner. AE, DISC, MC, V. Tues–Sun 11am–10pm (lunch menu until 3pm). Bus: Numerous Old Town routes including 8, 9, 10, 28, or 30. Trolley: Old Town.

★★★ **Bertrand at Mister A's** BALBOA PARK *AMERICAN/MEDITERRANEAN* A bar/patio menu gives diners on a budget access to a seasonal menu and million-dollar vistas. *2550 Fifth Ave. (at Laurel St.), Hillcrest.* ☎ 619/239-1377. www.bertrandatmisteras.com. Entrees $15–$30 lunch, $29–$50 dinner. AE, DC, MC, V. Mon–Fri 11:30am–2:30pm; Mon–Fri 5:30–9:30pm; Sat–Sun 5–9:30pm. Bus: 3 or 120.

The farm-to-table Arterra in Del Mar.

Bino's Bistro & Winebar CORONADO *BREAKFAST/LIGHT FARE* This casual, Euro-style spot serves sweet and savory crepes, fresh-baked bread and pastries, deli sandwiches, and salads. *1120 Adella Ave. (off Orange Ave.).* ☎ 619/522-0612. Entrees $6–$11. AE, DISC, MC, V. Daily 7am–5pm. Bus: 901 or 904.

★★ **Bite** HILLCREST *CALIFORNIAN* This stylishly modern bistro features a roster of seasonally driven small-plates that encourage grazing and sharing. *1417 University Ave. (at Richmond St.).* ☎ 619/299-2483. www.bitesd.com. Small plates $5–$16. AE, DC, MC, V. Daily 11am–10pm. Bus: 1, 10, or 11.

★★★ **Blanca** SOLANA BEACH *CALIFORNIAN/FRENCH* Sleek and sophisticated, this cosmopolitan space is one of the best restaurants in San Diego County and has a farm-to-table mindset. *437 S. Coast Hwy. 101 (north of Via de la Valle).* ☎ 858/792-0072. www.dineblanca.com. Entrees $17–$35; lounge menu $6–$22. AE, DC, DISC, MC, V. Mon–Thurs 5:30–9:30pm; Fri–Sat 5:30–10:30pm. Bus: 101.

★★ **Bread & Cie** HILLCREST *LIGHT FARE/MEDITERRANEAN* The traditions of European artisan bread-making are proudly carried on here. You can get a light breakfast or a great sandwich, as well as loaves of specialty breads. *350 University Ave. (at Fourth St.).* ☎ *619/683-9322. www. breadandcie.com. Sandwiches and light meals $4–$9. DISC, MC, V. Mon–Fri 7am–7pm; Sat 7am–6pm; Sun 8am–6pm. Bus: 1, 3, 10, 11, or 120.*

Brian's 24 Restaurant Bar & Grill GASLAMP QUARTER AMERICAN/ECLECTIC If you have a hankering for chicken and waffles at 3am, this surprisingly nice 24-hour restaurant has you covered. *828 Sixth Ave. (at F St.).* ☎ *619/702-8410. www.brians24.com. Entrees $10–$25. AE, DISC, MC, V. Open 24 hr. Bus: 3, 120, or 992.*

★ **Brockton Villa** LA JOLLA *BREAKFAST/CALIFORNIAN* A restored 1894 beach bungalow, this charming cafe occupies a breathtaking perch overlooking La Jolla Cove. *1235 Coast Blvd. (across from La Jolla Cove).* ☎ *858/454-7393. www.brocktonvilla. com. Entrees $8–$15 breakfast, $11–$16 lunch, $16–$30 dinner. AE, DISC, MC, V. Daily 8am–3pm; till 9pm for dinner June–Sept only. Bus: 30.*

★★ kids **Bronx Pizza** HILLCREST *ITALIAN* This tiny pizzeria serves up arguably San Diego's best pies—other than calzones, that's all it makes. There's usually a line out the door. *111 Washington St. (at First Ave.).* ☎ *619/291-3341. www.bronx pizza.com. Phone orders accepted for full pies. Pies $13–$19; $2.50 by the slice. Cash only. Sun–Thurs 11am–10pm; Fri–Sat 11am–11pm. Bus: 3, 10, or 83.*

★★ **Thee Bungalow** OCEAN BEACH *FRENCH* The fanciest restaurant in laid-back Ocean Beach. Features an excellent wine list and house specialties like *osso buco*–style lamb shank and dessert soufflés for two. *4996 W. Point Loma Blvd. (at Bacon St.).* ☎ *619/224-2884. www.cohnrestaurants.com. Entrees $23–$31. AE, DC, DISC, MC, V. Mon–Thurs 5:30–9:30pm; Fri–Sat 5–10pm; Sun 5–9pm. Bus: 35 or 923.*

★★ **Cafe Chloe** EAST VILLAGE *FRENCH* The conviviality of this bistro—combined with a short-but-sweet French-inspired menu covering breakfast, lunch, and dinner—makes for a winning dining experience. *721 Ninth Ave. (at G St.).* ☎ *619/232-3242. www.cafechloe.com. Entrees $8–$13 breakfast, $7–$18 lunch,*

Bread & Cie in Hillcrest.

Brockton Villa in La Jolla.

$15–$23 dinner. AE, MC, V. Mon–Fri 7:30am–10:30pm; Sat 8:30am–10:30pm; Sun 8:30am–9:30pm. Bus: 3, 5, 11, 901, or 929.

★★★ Candelas GASLAMP QUARTER/CORONADO *MEXICAN* If you're in the mood for a sophisticated, romantic fine-dining experience, look no further. The Coronado location has gorgeous views. *416 Third Ave. (at J St.), Gaslamp Quarter; 1201 First St. (at the Ferry Landing), Coronado.* ☎ *619/702-4455 Gaslamp Quarter,* ☎ *619/435-4900 Coronado. www. candelas-sd.com. Entrees $7–$16 breakfast and lunch, $18–$53 dinner. AE, DC, DISC, MC, V. Sat–Sun 8am–2pm; Mon–Fri 11am–2pm; daily 5–11pm. Gaslamp Quarter—Bus: 11 or 120; Trolley: Convention Center. Coronado—Bus: 901 or 904.*

★ Chez Loma CORONADO *FRENCH* Tables are scattered throughout this classic Victorian house and on the enclosed garden terrace; early birds enjoy specially priced meals—$25 for a three-course meal before 6pm (and all night on Tues). *1132 Loma (off Orange Ave.).* ☎ *619/435-0661. www.chezloma.com. Entrees $24–$37. AE, DC, DISC, MC, V. Tues–Sun 5–10pm. Bus: 901 or 904.*

★ The Cottage LA JOLLA *BREAKFAST/LIGHT FARE* Maybe La Jolla's best breakfast, served at a turn-of-the-20th-century bungalow on a shady corner. The house-made granola is a favorite. *7702 Fay Ave. (at Kline St.).* ☎ *858/454-8409. www. cottagelajolla.com. Entrees $8–$13 breakfast, $10–$16 lunch, $12–$23 dinner. AE, DISC, MC, V. Daily 7:30am–3pm; dinner (June–Aug only) Tues–Sat 5–9:30pm. Bus: 30.*

★★ Cowboy Star EAST VILLAGE *AMERICAN* This restaurant and butcher shop is an unabashed homage to classic Hollywood westerns,

Café Chloe in the East Village.

Candelas in the Gaslamp Quarter.

specializing in dry-aged meats and game fowl. *650 10th Ave. (btw. G and Market sts.).* ☎ *619/450-5880. www. thecowboystar.com. Entrees $10–$21 lunch, $19–$82 dinner. AE, DISC, MC, V. Lunch Tues–Fri 11:30am–2:30pm; dinner Tues–Thurs 5–10pm, Fri–Sat 5–10:30pm, Sun 5–9pm; bar menu Tues–Sun from 4pm. Bus: 3, 5, 11, 901, or 929. Trolley: Park & Market.*

★★★ Cucina Urbana BALBOA PARK *ITALIAN* One of the city's food-scene darlings, featuring rustic Italian fare that keeps one's pocketbook in mind while at no time sacrificing quality or creativity. *505 Laurel St. (at Fifth Ave.).* ☎ *619/239-2222. www.sdurbankitchen.com. Entrees $12–$20. AE, DISC, MC, V. Sun–Mon 5–9pm; Tues–Thurs 5–10pm; Fri–Sat 5–10:30pm (limited menu until midnight); lunch Tues–Fri 11:30am–2pm. Bus: 3 or 120.*

★ Dobson's Bar & Restaurant GASLAMP QUARTER *CALIFORNIAN* By day it buzzes with the energy of movers and shakers; in the evening it segues from happy-hour watering hole to sophisticated pre-theater American bistro. *956 Broadway Circle (at Broadway).* ☎ *619/231-6771. www.dobsonsrestaurant.com. Entrees $11–$20 lunch, $16–$39*

dinner. AE, MC, V. Mon–Fri 11:30am–10pm; Sat 3–10pm; happy hour Mon–Fri 4–6pm. Bus: Numerous downtown routes including 7, 929, or 992. Trolley: Civic Center.*

★★★ El Agave Tequileria OLD TOWN *MEXICAN* The regional Mexican cuisine and rustic elegance here leave the touristy joints of Old Town far behind. It also boasts more than 850 tequilas and mezcals, and some of the best margaritas in town. *2304 San Diego Ave. (at Old Town Ave.).* ☎ *619/220-0692. www. elagave.com. Entrees $8–$11 lunch, $16–$32 dinner. AE, MC, V. Daily 11am–10pm. Bus: Numerous routes including 8, 9, 10, 28, or 30. Trolley: Old Town.*

★ El Camino LITTLE ITALY *MEXICAN* This hipster cantina serves simple Mexican fare like open-face tacos created from organic products. It's also a casual nightspot with live music and DJs. *2400 India St. (at W. Kalmia St.).* ☎ *619/685-3881. www. elcaminosd.com. Entrees $9–$14. AE, MC, V. Mon 5–10pm; Tues–Sat 5–11pm; Sun 10am–10pm; bar open nightly until 1 or 2am. Bus: 83.*

★★★ Extraordinary Desserts HILLCREST/LITTLE ITALY *DESSERTS/ LIGHT FARE* Dozens of divine creations are available daily; there's also an exclusive line of jams, syrups, spices, and confections for sale. The Little Italy location serves panini, salads, cheese, and alcohol; the Hillcrest outpost serves desserts only. *2929 Fifth Ave. (btw. Palm and Quince sts.), Hillcrest; 1430 Union St. (btw. Beech and Ash sts.), Little Italy.* ☎ *619/294-2132 Hillcrest;* ☎ *619/294-7001 Little Italy. www.extraordinarydesserts. com. Desserts $2–$9; salads and sandwiches $8–$18. AE, MC, V. Mon–Thurs 8:30am–11pm; Fri 8:30am–midnight; Sat 10am–midnight; Sun 10am–11pm. Hillcrest—Bus: 3 or 120. Little Italy—Bus: 30.*

★ kids Filippi's Pizza Grotto

LITTLE ITALY *ITALIAN* Walk through an Italian grocery and deli to get to the dining room, where the menu offers more than 15 pizzas, plus huge portions of pasta. *1747 India St. (btw. Date and Fir sts.).* ☎ *619/232-5094. www.realcheesepizza.com. Entrees $6–$13. AE, DC, DISC, MC, V. Sun–Mon 11am–10pm; Tues–Thurs 11am–10:30pm; Fri–Sat 11am–11:30pm; deli opens daily at 8am. Bus: 83. Trolley: County Center/Little Italy. Other location: Pacific Beach, 962 Garnet Ave. (btw. Cass and Bayard sts.),* ☎ *858/483-6222, Bus: 8/9.*

Dobson's Bar & Restaurant in the Gaslamp Quarter.

★ The Fishery PACIFIC BEACH

SEAFOOD You're pretty well guaranteed fresh-off-the-boat seafood at this off-the-beaten-track establishment. It's really a wholesale warehouse and retail fish market with a casual restaurant attached. *5040 Cass St. (at Opal St.).* ☎ *858/272-9985. www.pacshell.com. Entrees $9–$28 lunch, $10–$35 dinner. AE, DC, DISC, MC, V. Daily 11am–10pm. Bus: 30.*

★ The Fish Market/Top of the Market EMBARCADERO *SEAFOOD/SUSHI*

This view-enhanced, always-packed restaurant is a San Diego institution. Upstairs, fancy Top of the Market offers sea fare with souped-up presentations. *750 N. Harbor Dr.* ☎ *619/232-3474. www.thefishmarket.com. Entrees $10–$63 lunch, $13–$71 dinner (Top of the Market main courses $12–$75 lunch, $17–$95 dinner). AE, DC, DISC, MC, V. Daily 11am–10pm. Trolley: Seaport Village. Other location: Del Mar, 640 Via de la Valle (btw. S. Cedros Ave. and Solana Circle E),* ☎ *858/755-2277.*

★★★ Georges California Modern LA JOLLA *CALIFORNIAN*

This place has it all: stunning ocean views, style, impeccable service,

El Agave Tequileria in Old Town.

and above all, a world-class chef. Those seeking fine food and incomparable views at more modest prices can head upstairs to Georges Ocean Terrace and George's Bar. *1250 Prospect St. (east of Ivanhoe Ave.).* ☎ *858/454-4244. www.georgesatthecove.com. Entrees $28–$90. AE, DC, DISC, MC, V. Sun–Thurs 5:30–10pm; Fri–Sat 5–10pm. Ocean Terrace entrees $10–$15 lunch, $17–$25 dinner. Daily 11am–10pm (Fri–Sat till 10:30pm). Bus: 30.*

★ **Gringo's** PACIFIC BEACH *MEXICAN* The menu at this upscale space runs the gamut from the typical fare to regional specialties from Oaxaca, the Yucatan, and Mexico's Pacific Coast. More than 100 tequilas available. *4474 Mission Blvd. (at Garnet Ave.).* ☎ *858/490-2877. www.gringoscantina.com. Entrees $6–$14 lunch, $8–$31 dinner, $17–$20 Sun brunch. AE, DC, DISC, MC, V. Mon–Sat 11am–11pm; Sun 9am–11pm. Bus: 8/9, 27, or 30.*

★★ **Island Prime** EMBARCADERO *SEAFOOD* With its spectacular bay and skyline vistas, it would be easy to understand if Island Prime didn't even bother to make its food interesting—but the views actually have some competition here. *880 Harbor Island Dr.* ☎ *619/298-6802. www.*

Extraordinary Desserts in Little Italy.

cohnrestaurants.com. Entrees $11–$29 lunch, $25–$49 dinner. AE, DC, DISC, MC, V. Sun–Thurs 11:30am–10pm; Fri–Sat 11:30am–11pm. Bus: 923 or 992.

★ **Jake's Del Mar** DEL MAR *SEAFOOD/CALIFORNIAN* This seafood-and-view restaurant has a perfect seat next to the sand—the predictable menu can't live up to the panorama, but it's prepared competently. *1660 Coast Blvd. (at 15th St.).* ☎ *858/755-2002. www.jakesdelmar.com. Entrees $10–$18 lunch, $17–$53 dinner, $11–$17 brunch. AE, DISC, MC, V. Tues–Sat 11:30am–2:30pm; Sun brunch 10am–2pm; daily 5–9pm (Fri–Sat till 9:30pm). Bus: 101.*

★★ **The Linkery** NORTH PARK *AMERICAN* This farm-to-table hot spot specializes in house-made sausages, meat and cheese boards, and grilled flatbreads; there are vegetarian and vegan options, too. *3794 30th St. (at North Park Way).* ☎ *619/255-8778. www.thelinkery.com. Entrees $10–$29. AE, DC, DISC, MC, V. Mon–Thurs 5:30–11:30pm; Fri–Sat noon–11:30pm; Sun 11am–11:30pm. Bus: 2, 6, 7, or 10.*

★★★ **The Marine Room** LA JOLLA *FRENCH/CALIFORNIAN* This shorefront institution has been San Diego's most celebrated dining room since 1941. Executive chef Bernard Guillas sees to it that the food lives up to its room with a view. *2000 Spindrift Dr. (at Torrey Pines Rd.).* ☎ *866/644-2351. www.marineroom.com. Entrees $27–$48. AE, DC, DISC, MC, V. Sun–Thurs 5:30–9pm; Fri–Sat 5:30–10pm; lounge daily from 4pm. Bus: 30.*

★★★ **Market Restaurant + Bar** DEL MAR *CALIFORNIAN/SUSHI* This comfortably elegant restaurant specializes in a regional San Diego cuisine, showcasing the best ingredients from the area's top farms, ranches, and seafood providers. *3702 Via de la Valle (at El Camino*

Real). ☎ 858/523-0007. *www.market delmar.com. Entrees $25–$35; sushi $12–$22. AE, MC, V. Daily 5–10pm. Bus: 308.*

★★★ **Nine-Ten** LA JOLLA *CALIFORNIAN* The seasonal menu at this stylish spot is best enjoyed via small-plate grazing; better yet, turn yourself over to the "Mercy of the Chef" tasting menu. *910 Prospect St. (btw. Fay and Girard aves.).* ☎ 858/964-5400. *www.nine-ten.com. Entrees $6–$18 breakfast, $11–$18 lunch, $13–$40 dinner. AE, DC, DISC, MC, V. Daily 6:30–11am (Sun until 12:30pm), 11:30am–2:30pm, and 6–10pm. Bus: 30.*

★★ **Nobu** GASLAMP QUARTER SUSHI/ASIAN FUSION Celebrity-approved fare from chef Nobu Matsuhisa. This place is pricey and has a full-volume ambience, but it's hard to argue with the textures, flavors, and beautiful presentations. *207 Fifth Ave. (at L St. in the Hard Rock Hotel).* ☎ 619/814-4124. *www.nobu restaurants.com. Entrees $29–$96; sushi $6–$14. AE, DC, DISC, MC, V. Sun–Thurs 5:30–10pm; Fri–Sat 5:30–11pm; lounge Mon–Fri 5–10:30pm, Sat 5pm–1am, Sun 5–11:30pm. Bus: 3, 11, or 120. Trolley: Gaslamp Quarter.*

★★ **The Oceanaire Seafood Room** GASLAMP QUARTER *SEAFOOD* Featuring top local products as well as fish brought in daily from around the globe, the menu incorporates elements of Pacific Rim, Italian, classic French, and Asian cuisine. *400 J St. (at Fourth Ave.).* ☎ 619/858-2277. *www.the oceanaire.com. Entrees $15–$60. AE, DISC, MC, V. Sun–Thurs 5–10pm; Fri–Sat 5–11pm. Bus: 3, 11, or 120. Trolley: Convention Center.*

★★ **Red Pearl Kitchen** GASLAMP QUARTER *CHINESE/ASIAN FUSION* This sexy restaurant and bar specializes in dim sum dishes with a

Island Prime in the Embarcadero.

contemporary, Pan Asian flair. *440 J St. (btw. Fourth and Fifth aves.).* ☎ 619/231-1100. *www.redpearl kitchen.com. Entrees $8–$23. AE, MC, V. Sun–Wed 5–10pm; Thurs–Fri 5–11pm; Sat 5pm–1am. Bus: 3, 11, or 120. Trolley: Gaslamp Quarter or Convention Center.*

★ **Roppongi** LA JOLLA *ASIAN FUSION/PACIFIC RIM* The cuisines of Japan, Thailand, China, Vietnam, Korea, and India collide, via a menu of tapas-style portions designed for sharing. *875 Prospect St. (at Fay Ave.).* ☎ 858/551-5252. *www. roppongiusa.com. Entrees $11–$19 lunch, $9–$19 tapas, $23–$48 dinner. AE, DC, DISC, MC, V. Sun–Thurs 11:30am–9:30pm; Fri–Sat 11:30am–10:30pm. Bus: 30.*

★★★ **Sushi Ota** PACIFIC BEACH *SUSHI* Masterful chef-owner Yukito Ota creates San Diego's finest sushi in a nondescript location in a mini-mall. Discerning regulars look for the daily specials posted behind the counter. *4529 Mission Bay Dr. (at Bunker Hill).* ☎ 858/270-5670. *Entrees $6–$14 lunch, $9–$22 dinner; sushi $4–$13. AE, MC, V. Tues–Fri 11:30am–2pm and 5:30–10:30pm; Sat–Sun 5–10:30pm. Bus: 30.*

★★★ **Tapenade** LA JOLLA *FRENCH* The fresh, sunny fare helped redefine French cuisine in San Diego. This elegant, distinguished restaurant is a

Red Pearl Kitchen in the Gaslamp Quarter.

poster child for the giant leap local dining has taken over the last decade. *7612 Fay Ave. (btw. Kline and Pearl sts.).* ☎ *858/551-7500. www.tapenaderestaurant.com. Entrees $14–$19 lunch, $26–$38 dinner. AE, MC, V. Tues–Fri 11:30am–2:30pm; Sun–Thurs 5:30–9:30pm; Fri–Sat 5:30–10pm. Bus: 30.*

★★ **The Tractor Room** HILL-CREST AMERICAN   Game meats like rabbit, venison, and boar, as well as manly cuts of steak are prominently featured. There's also a massive selection of scotch, whiskey, and bourbon. *3687 Fifth Ave. (at Pennsylvania Ave.).* ☎ *619/543-1007. www. thetractorroom.com. Entrees $15–$36. AE, DISC, MC, V. Mon–Thurs 5pm–midnight (kitchen until 11:30pm); Fri 5pm–2am (kitchen until 11:30pm); Sat 9am–2pm and 5pm–2am (kitchen until midnight); Sun 9am–2pm and 5pm–midnight (kitchen until 11:30pm). Bus: 3 or 120.*

★★ **Urban Solace** NORTH PARK AMERICAN   This loud and cheerful eatery will speed you to a happy place with its creative, contemporary take on American comfort food. The bluegrass Sunday brunch keeps the good times rolling. *3823 30th St. (at University Ave.).* ☎ *619/295-6465.*

www.urbansolace.net. Entrees $9–$16 lunch, $14–$20 dinner. Mon–Thurs 11:30am–10pm; Fri–Sat 11:30am–11pm; Sun 10am–2:45pm and 5–9pm. Bus: 2, 6, 7, or 10.

★★ **Whisknladle** LA JOLLA CALI-FORNIAN   Gourmet comfort food created from top-quality ingredients at modest sums, and retail pricing on wine. Late-night lounge and cocktail scene on Friday and Saturday. *1044 Wall St. (at Hershel Ave.).* ☎ *858/551-7575. www.whisknladle. com. Entrees $11–$32 lunch, $15–$32 dinner. AE, DISC, MC, V. Sun–Thurs 11:30am–9pm; Fri–Sat 11:30am–10pm (lounge until 1:30am). Bus: 30.*

★★ **Zenbu** LA JOLLA SUSHI/SEA-FOOD   You can order something from the sushi bar or maybe an entree like steak of locally har-pooned swordfish—caught by the restaurant owner's personal fishing fleet. There's also a second location in Cardiff-by-the-Sea. *7660 Fay Ave. (at Kline St.).* ☎ *858/454-4540. www.zenbusushi.com. Entrees $22–$30. AE, DC, DISC, MC, V. Sun–Wed 5–10:30pm; Thurs–Sat 5–11:30pm; lounge Thurs–Sat 8pm–1am. Bus: 30. Other location: Cardiff-by-the-Sea, 2003 San Elijo Ave. (at Birmingham Dr.).* ☎ *760/633-2233.* ●

Nightlife Best Bets

Best Bar with a View
★★★ Top of the Hyatt *1 Market Pl.* (p 118)

Best Concert Venue (Indoor)
★★★ Belly Up Tavern *143 S. Cedros Ave. (p 120)*

Best Concert Venue (Outdoor)
★★ Humphrey's *2241 Shelter Island Dr. (p 121)*

Best Rock-'n'-Roll Club
★★ The Casbah *2501 Kettner Blvd.* (p 120)

Best Jazz Club
★ Dizzy's *200 Harbor Dr. (p 120)*

Best Dive Bar
★ Nunu's *3537 Fifth Ave. (p 118)*

Best Wine Bar
★★★ 3rd Corner *2265 Bacon St.* (p 122)

Best Megaclub
★★ Stingaree *454 Sixth Ave.* (p 122)

Best Shoes-Optional Bar
★★ Beach *421 B St. (p 117)*

Best Open-Air Bar (High-Rise)
★★ Altitude Sky Lounge *660 K St.* (p 117)

Best Open-Air Bar (Low-Rise)
★★ Lounge Six *616 J St. (p 117)*

Best Place to Pick Up a Spare
East Village Tavern & Bowl *930 Market St. (p 117)*

Best Supper Club
★★★ Anthology *1337 India St. (p 121)*

Best 2-for-1 Experience
★★ The Onyx Room/Thin *852 Fifth Ave. (p 118)*

Best Art Collection
★★★ House of Blues *1055 Fifth Ave. (p 121)*

Coolest Pool Room
★★ On Broadway *615 Broadway* (p 119)

Best Spot for Latin Music
★★ Sevilla *555 Fourth Ave. (p 122)*

Best Drag Revue
★ Lips *3036 El Cajon Blvd. (p 121)*

Best Goth Fun House
★★ Voyeur *755 Fifth Ave. (p 119)*

Previous page: Gaslamp Quarter.

Downtown Nightlife

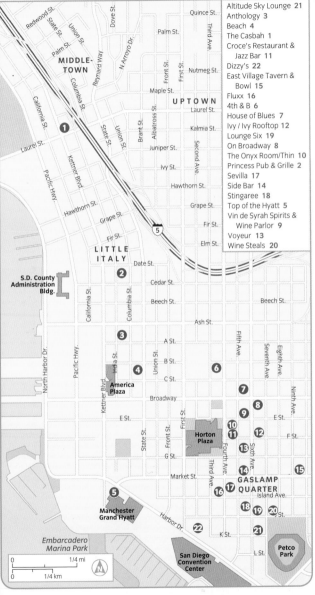

Hillcrest Nightlife

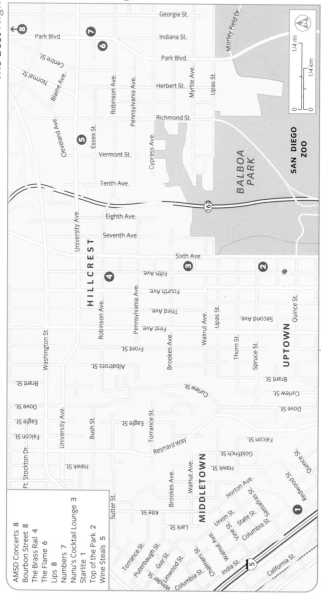

Beaches Nightlife

Bar West **2**
Belly Up Tavern **1**
Humphrey's **6**
Sound Wave **3**
3rd Corner **5**
The Vine **4**

Nightlife A to Z

Bars

★★ Altitude Sky Lounge

GASLAMP QUARTER   Twenty-two stories up in a Marriott hotel, this long, narrow open-air space looks down on PETCO Park and the Convention Center. *660 K St. (btw. 6th and 7th aves.).* ☎ *619/696-0234. www. atltitudeskybar.com. No cover. Bus: 3, 11, 120, or 992. Trolley: Orange Line to Gaslamp Quarter. Map p 115.*

★★ **Beach** DOWNTOWN   This is the rooftop bar of the W hotel. Go ahead and kick off your shoes—the sand is heated. The hotel's two other bars, Living Room and Access, are also stylish venues. *421 B St. (at State St.).* ☎ *619/398-3100. www.wbeach bar.com. No cover. Bus: All Broadway*

routes. Trolley: Blue or Orange Line to America Plaza. Map p 115.

East Village Tavern & Bowl

EAST VILLAGE   Featuring 12 colorfully lit bowling lanes, as well as billiards and a separate bar area with outdoor seating, this raucous place has classic bar food and a good selection of brews on tap. Kids are allowed in until 9pm. *930 Market St. (btw. Ninth and 10th aves.).* ☎ *619/677-2695. www.bowlevt.com. No cover. Bus: 3 or 11. Trolley: Gaslamp Quarter or Park and Market. Map p 115.*

★★ **Lounge Six** GASLAMP QUARTER   On the fourth-floor pool deck of the Hotel Solamar, there are fire pits, cabanas, comfy lounges, and views of the Gaslamp Quarter action. *616 J St.*

Altitude Sky Lounge in the Gaslamp Quarter.

(at Sixth Ave.). ☎ 619/531-8744. www.hotelsolamar.com. No cover. Bus: 3 or 120. Trolley: Orange Line to Gaslamp Quarter. Map p 115.

★ **Nunu's Cocktail Lounge** HILL-CREST   Lots of 1960s Naugahyde style, plus cheap drinks and a kitchen that whips up specialties like the Jack Daniel's burger for an eclectic crowd. *3537 Fifth Ave. (at Ivy Lane).* ☎ 619/ 295-2878. No cover. Bus: 3 or 120. Map p 116.

★★ **The Onyx Room/Thin** GASLAMP QUARTER   At street level is hyper-modern Thin, where cocktails mix with DJ grooves; subterranean Onyx is a classic lounge, featuring diverse live music

Ivy Rooftop at the Andaz San Diego.

Wednesday and Thursday. *852 Fifth Ave. (btw. E and F sts.).* ☎ 619/235-6699. www.onyxroom.com. Cover Fri–Sat $10–$15 (covers both bars). Bus: 3, 120, 992, or any Broadway route. Trolley: Fifth Ave. Map p 115.

★ **Princess Pub & Grille** LITTLE ITALY   A local haunt for Anglophiles and others hankering for a pint o' Watney's and some bangers 'n' mash. *1665 India St. (at Date St.).* ☎ 619/702-3021. www.princesspub. com. No cover. Bus: 83. Trolley: Blue Line to County Center/Little Italy. Map p 115.

★★ **Side Bar** GASLAMP QUARTER Ornate fixtures, dangling vintage bird cages, and erotic art add to the Victorian bordello feeling at this small, sexy lounge and nightclub. *536 Market St. (at Sixth Ave.).* ☎ 619/ 696-0946. www.sidebarsd.com. Cover none–$15. Bus: 3 or 11. Trolley: Gaslamp Quarter. Map p 115.

★★★ **Top of the Hyatt** EMBARCADERO   On the 40th floor of the West Coast's tallest waterfront building, this is San Diego's ultimate bar with a view. *1 Market Place (at Harbor Dr.).* ☎ 619/232-1234. www. manchestergrand.hyatt.com. No cover. Trolley: Orange Line to Seaport Village. Map p 115.

Dance Clubs

Bar West PACIFIC BEACH   With its bottle service, VIP booths, and dinner service, Bar West brings some downtown chic (and attitude) to the beach. *959 Hornblend St. (btw. Cass and Bayard sts.).* ☎ *858/273-4800. www.barwestsd.com. Cover $5–$10. Bus: 8/9. Map p 117.*

★ FLUXX GASLAMP QUARTER
If you can make it past the doorman you'll be wowed by the state-of-the-art sound and lighting and Vegas-style glitz at this upscale club. Themes change monthly, hence the name. *500 Fourth Ave. (btw. Island Ave. and Market St.).* ☎ *619/232-8100. www.fluxxsd.com. Cover $15–$20. Bus: 3, 11, or 120. Trolley: Convention Center.*

★★★ Ivy/Ivy Rooftop GASLAMP QUARTER   Multilevel Ivy is chic and sexy with a definite A-lister vibe; Ivy Rooftop is an open-air bar where beautiful people prove a distraction to the beautiful views. *600 F St. (btw. Sixth and Seventh aves. at the Andaz Hotel).* ☎ *619/814-2055. www.envysandiego.com. Cover $10–$20. Bus: 3 or 120. Trolley: Gaslamp Quarter. Map p 115.*

★★ On Broadway GASLAMP QUARTER   This dress-to-impress hangout in an old bank has five rooms covering the musical gamut, plus a sushi bar, and a billiards room in the former vault. *615 Broadway (at Sixth Ave.).* ☎ *619/231-0011. www.obec.tv. Cover $15–$25. Bus: All Broadway routes. Trolley: Blue or Orange Line to Fifth Ave. Map p 115.*

★★ Voyeur GASLAMP QUARTER
This Goth fun house features AK-47-shaped lamps, skull motifs, and go-go dancers embedded in a floor-to-ceiling wall of pulsing light. The club pulls top talent to man the decks. *755 Fifth Ave. (btw. F and G sts.).* ☎ *619/756-7678. www.voyeur*

Bourbon Street in University Heights.

sd.com. Cover none–$30. Bus: 3, 120, or 992. Trolley: Fifth Ave. Map p 115.

Gay & Lesbian Bars & Clubs

★★ Bourbon Street UNIVERSITY HEIGHTS   There's an outdoor patio, a game room for darts or pool, a performance area for open-mic nights and contests, and a lounge where DJs spin house music. Sunday is all about the girls. *4612 Park Blvd. (near Adams Ave.).* ☎ *619/291-4043. www.bourbonstreetsd.com. Bus: 11. Map p 116.*

★ The Brass Rail HILLCREST
San Diego's oldest gay bar, it's been remodeled and refreshed, and now features VIP rooms and bottle service. Every 2nd, 3rd, and 4th Friday is ladies night. *3796 Fifth Ave. (at Robinson St.).* ☎ *619/298-2233. www.thebrassrailsd.com. Cover $3–$15. Bus: 1, 3, or 120. Map p 116.*

★★ The Flame HILLCREST   An ever-changing roster of events—from comedy and magic to DJs—for both guys and gals. Happy hour is Friday to Sunday from 1 to 9pm. *3780 Park Blvd. (at Robinson Ave.).* ☎ *619/795-8578. www.flamesandiego.com. Covers vary. Bus: 1, 7, 10, or 11. Map p 116.*

★★ Numbers HILLCREST   It's a predominantly male crowd at this busy dance emporium, just across the street from The Flame. *3811 Park*

Anthology in Little Italy.

Blvd. (at University Ave.). ☎ 619/ 294-7583. www.numbers-sd.com. Cover $3–$10. Bus: 1, 7, 10, or 11. Map p 116.

★★★ Top of the Park HILLCREST The weekend party scene officially begins here at the penthouse bar of the Park Manor Hotel, Friday evenings from 5 to 10pm. *525 Spruce St. (at Fifth Ave.).* ☎ *619/291-0999. www.parkmanorsuites.com. No cover. Bus: 3 or 120. Map p 116.*

Live Music Venues

★ 4th & B DOWNTOWN   In a former bank building, this venue has great sound and eclectic booking— everything from comedy to a wide range of musical artists. *345 B St. (at Fourth Ave.).* ☎ *619/231-4343. www.4thandBevents.com. Ticket*

Stingaree in the Gaslamp Quarter.

prices vary. Bus: 3, 120, 850, or 860. Trolley: Civic Center. Map p 115.

★ AMSD Concerts NORMAL HEIGHTS   One of San Diego's most unique venues is this nearly 100-year-old church. The nonreligious programming includes Americana, blues, Celtic, and bluegrass. *4650 Mansfield St. (at Adams Ave.).* ☎ *619/303-8176. www.amsd concerts.com. $20–$45 (dinner packages available). Bus: 11. Map p 116.*

★★★ Belly Up Tavern SOLANA BEACH   A 30-minute drive from downtown, this funky beach bar hosts international artists of all genres and is arguably San Diego's best spot for live music. *143 S. Cedros Ave. (south of Lomas Santa Fe Dr.).* ☎ *858/481-9022 (recorded info) or 858/481-8140 (box office). www.bellyup.com. $15–$25. Bus: 101. Map p 117.*

★★ The Casbah LITTLE ITALY This rockin' club has a well-earned rep for showcasing alternative and punk bands that either are, were, or will be famous; live music can be counted on at least 6 nights a week. *2501 Kettner Blvd. (at Laurel St.).* ☎ *619/232-4355. www.casbahmusic. com. Cover charge usually under $15. Bus: 83. Map p 115.*

★ Dizzy's GASLAMP QUARTER This is where you'll find uncompromising, straight-ahead jazz; the all-ages venue is in the San Diego Wine & Culinary Center. *200 Harbor Dr. (at Second Ave.).* ☎ 858/270-7467. www.dizzyssandiego.com. *$10–$15 (tickets available at the door; cash only). Bus: 992. Trolley: Convention Center. Map p 115.*

★★ **Humphrey's** SHELTER ISLAND This locally beloved 1,300-seat outdoor venue is alongside the water next to bobbing sailboats. An indoor lounge, Humphrey's Backstage, also has music nightly. *2241 Shelter Island Dr.* ☎ 619/523-1010 (general info) or 619-224-3577 (reservations). www. humphreysconcerts.com. *Ticket prices vary. Bus: 28. Map p 117.*

Sound Wave MISSION BEACH A killer beachfront location, right alongside the Mission Beach amusement park. There's indoor/outdoor dining, three bars, and a 700-person capacity music venue. *3105 Ocean Front Walk (at Mission Blvd. and W. Mission Bay Dr.).* ☎ 858/320-2100. www. wavehousesandiego.com. *Ticket prices vary. Bus: 8/9. Map p 117.*

Supper Clubs

★★★ **Anthology** LITTLE ITALY Acoustically excellent and architecturally alluring supper club featuring a host of marquee-name jazz, blues, rock, and world music artists. Diners get the best seats. *1337 India St.*

(btw. Ash and A sts.). ☎ 619/595-0300. www.anthologysd.com. *Tickets usually $15–$45; $15 minimum food/beverage for 1st floor and mezzanine. Bus: 83. Map p 115.*

★★ **Croce's Restaurant & Jazz Bar** GASLAMP QUARTER A lively, mainstream place where you'll find a variety of jazz and rhythm and blues 7 nights a week. *802 Fifth Ave. (at F St.).* ☎ 619/233-4355. www. croces.com. *Cover $5–$10 (cover is waived if you eat at the restaurant). Bus: 3, 120, or 992. Map p 115.*

★★★ **House of Blues** DOWN-TOWN Filled with cool art, there are two stages and a restaurant serving Southern-inspired cuisine (also open for lunch and Sun Gospel brunch). *1055 Fifth Ave. (btw. Broadway and C St.).* ☎ 619/299-2583. www.hob.com/sandiego. *Ticket prices vary. Bus: 3, 120, or numerous Broadway routes. Trolley: Fifth Ave. Map p 115.*

★ **Lips** NORTH PARK This drag revue has a different show nightly, such as Bitchy Bingo on Wednesday and celebrity impersonations on Thursday; Sunday there's a Gospel brunch. Weekend late shows are 21 and over only. *3036 El Cajon Blvd. (at 30th St.).* ☎ 619/295-7900. www.lips show.biz. *Cover $3–$5; food minimum $10–$15. Bus: 1 or 15. Map p 116.*

3rd Corner in Ocean Beach.

★★ **Starlite** MIDDLETOWN This hip restaurant and bar eschews the large-scale dine-and-dance scene that's popular in the Gaslamp Quarter for an intimate, mondo-exotica lounge feel. *3175 India St. (at Spruce St.).* ☎ *619/358-9766. www.starlite sandiego.com. No cover. Bus: 83. Trolley: Blue Line to Middletown. Map p 116.*

★★ **Sevilla** GASLAMP QUARTER This Spanish-themed club is the place for salsa and merengue lessons; there's also a tapas bar and dining room. Live flamenco dinner shows are staged Friday through Saturday. *555 Fourth Ave. (at Market St.).* ☎ *619/233-5979. www.cafe sevilla.com or sevillanightclub.com. Cover $5–$15. Bus: 3, 11, or 120. Trolley: Convention Center. Map p 115.*

★★ **Stingaree** GASLAMP QUARTER This three-level club has more than 22,000 square feet (2,044 sq. m) of space, a fine dining component, a handful of bars and private nooks, and a rooftop deck with cabanas and fire pit. *454 Sixth Ave. (btw. Island Ave. and J St.).* ☎ *619/544-9500. www.stingsandiego.com. Cover $20.*

Wine Steals in Hillcrest.

Trolley: Orange Line to Gaslamp Quarter. Map p 115.

Wine Bars

★★★ **3rd Corner** OCEAN BEACH This convivial wine bar multitasks as a restaurant and as a wine shop where you can meander through racks of wines looking for the right one to uncork. *2265 Bacon St. (btw. Voltaire St. and W. Point Loma Blvd.).* ☎ *619/223-2700. www. the3rdcorner.com. Bus: 35 or 923. Map p 117.*

★★ **Vin de Syrah Spirits & Wine Parlor** GASLAMP QUARTER This hot spot has a hidden, speakeasy entrance and an oddball Alice in Wonderland decor. It morphs into a jamming club Friday and Saturday nights. *901 Fifth Ave. (at E St.).* ☎ *619/234-4166. www.syrahwine parlor.com. Bus: 3, 120, or numerous Broadway routes. Trolley: Fifth Ave. Map p 115.*

★★ **The Vine** OCEAN BEACH Wine and beer drinkers can find common ground here—there's a great selection of suds, as well as an eclectic menu of small-plate offerings. *1851 Bacon St. (at Niagara Ave.).* ☎ *619/222-8463. www. theobvine.com. Bus: 35 or 923. Map p 117.*

★★ **Wine Steals** EAST VILLAGE/ HILLCREST This small franchise features a retail component and has four locations, including one just beyond the warning track at PETCO Park and a casual neighborhood spot in Hillcrest. *793–795 J St. (at Eighth Ave.), East Village.* ☎ *619/255-7452; 1243 University Ave. (btw. Richmond and Vermont sts.), Hillcrest,* ☎ *619/295-1188. www.winestealssd.com. Bus: 3, 11, 901, or 929; Trolley: Gaslamp Quarter (East Village). Bus: 1, 10, or 11 (Hillcrest). Map p 115.* ●

A&E **Best Bets**

Best **Classical Music Festival**
★★★ La Jolla Music Society
SummerFest *various locations*
(p 126)

Best **Sports Venue**
★★★ San Diego Padres' PETCO
Park *100 Park Blvd.* (p 129)

Best **Goal-Oriented Kicks**
★★ San Diego Sockers *2260 Jimmy
Durante Blvd.* (p 129)

Best **Place for Culture in a Mall**
★★ San Diego Repertory Theatre
Horton Plaza (p 130)

Best **Place for Foreign and
Indie Films**
★★ Hillcrest Cinema *3965 Fifth
Ave.* (p 127)

Most **Extreme Screen**
★★★ Fleet Science Center IMAX
Dome Theater *Balboa Park* (p 127)

Best **Restored Venues**
★★★ Birch North Park Theatre
2891 University Ave. (p 126); and

★★★ Balboa Theatre *868 Fourth
Ave.* (p 126)

Best **Use of Strings and
Pyrotechnics**
★★ San Diego Symphony Summer
Pops *Embarcadero Marina Park
South* (p 126)

Best **Broadway-Bound Fare**
★★★ La Jolla Playhouse *2910 La
Jolla Village Dr.* (p 129)

Best **Place to be a Groundling**
★★★ The Old Globe Theatre
Balboa Park (p 130)

Best **Place to Get Your
Dance On**
★★ Dance Place at NTC Promenade
2650 Truxton Rd. (p 126)

Best **Place for Tragic Heroines**
★★★ San Diego Opera *1200 Third
Ave.* (p 127)

Best **Place for Horsing Around**
★★★ Del Mar Races *2260 Jimmy
Durante Blvd.* (p 128)

Del Mar Race Track.

Previous page: PETCO Park, home of the San Diego Padres.

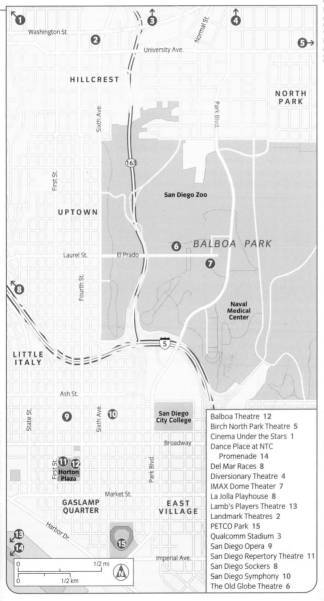

Balboa Theatre 12
Birch North Park Theatre 5
Cinema Under the Stars 1
Dance Place at NTC
    Promenade 14
Del Mar Races 8
Diversionary Theatre 4
IMAX Dome Theater 7
La Jolla Playhouse 8
Lamb's Players Theatre 13
Landmark Theatres 2
PETCO Park 15
Qualcomm Stadium 3
San Diego Opera 9
San Diego Repertory Theatre 11
San Diego Sockers 8
San Diego Symphony 10
The Old Globe Theatre 6

A&E **A to Z**

Classical Music

★★★ La Jolla Music Society

VARIOUS LOCATIONS   This well-respected organization has been bringing marquee names to San Diego since 1968; the annual SummerFest in August is always highly anticipated, featuring concerts, lectures, and workshops. *Performances at Sherwood Auditorium at the Museum of Contemporary Art in La Jolla, Neurosciences Institute, Copley Symphony Hall, and Birch North Park Theatre.* ☎ 858/459-3728. www.ljms.org. Tickets $25–$75.

★★ San Diego Symphony

DOWNTOWN/EMBARCADERO Top talent performs at Copley Symphony Hall, then transfers to the waterfront for an open-air summer pops season. *Symphony Hall, 750 B St. (at Seventh Ave.). Bus: Numerous Broadway routes. Trolley: Blue or Orange Line to 5th Ave.; Embarcadero Marina Park South (behind the Convention Center). Trolley: Orange Line to Gaslamp Quarter.* ☎ 619/235-0804. www.sandiego symphony.com. Tickets $20–$100.

The San Diego Symphony, downtown.

Concert & Performance Venues

★★★ Balboa Theatre GASLAMP

QUARTER   A gilded 1924 beauty spared from the wrecking ball and reopened in 2008, this downtown icon is once again presenting music, dance, theater, and film. *868 Fourth Ave. (btw. E and F sts.).* ☎ 619/570-1100 or 619/615-4000. www.sd balboa.org. Bus: 3, 120, or all Broadway routes. Trolley: Fifth Ave.

★★★ Birch North Park Theatre

NORTH PARK   This gloriously restored vaudeville house is home to Lyric Opera San Diego and also hosts a variety of performances and film presentations by other groups. *2891 University Ave. (at Kansas St.).* ☎ 619/239-8836 or 619/231-5714. www.birchnorthparktheatre.net. Ticket prices vary. Bus: 2, 6, 7, or 10.

Dance

★★ Dance Place at NTC Promenade POINT LOMA   This former

military base is now the heart of the city's dance scene, providing studio, performance, and educational space for San Diego Ballet (☎ 619/294-7378; www.sandiegoballet.org), Malashock Dance (☎ 619/260-1622; www.malashockdance.org), and Jean Isaacs San Diego Dance Theater (☎ 619/225-1803; www.sandiego dancetheater.org). *2650 Truxton Rd. (at Dewey Rd.).* ☎ 619/573-9260. www.ntcpromenade.org. Bus: 28. Map p 125.

Film

★★ Cinema Under the Stars

MISSION HILLS   An intimate, outdoor moviegoing experience that runs from spring through fall, featuring both classic and new releases. You can lounge in zero-gravity

What a Deal

Half-price tickets to theater, music, and dance events are available at the ARTS TIX booth in Horton Plaza Park, at Broadway and Third avenues. The kiosk is open Tuesday through Thursday at 11am, Friday to Sunday at 10am. The booth stays open until 6pm daily except Sunday, when it closes at 5pm. Half-price tickets are available only for same-day shows, except for Monday performances, which are sold on Sunday. For a daily listing of offerings, call ☎ 619/497-5000 or check www.sandiegoperforms.com; the website also sells half-price tickets for some shows. Full-price advance tickets are also available—the booth doubles as a Ticketmaster outlet.

chairs or sit at cafe tables. *4040 Goldfinch St. (at Fort Stockton Dr.).* ☎ *619/295-4221. www.topspresents. com. Tickets $14. Bus: 10 or 83. Map p 125.*

★★★ kids IMAX Dome Theater
BALBOA PARK The Reuben H. Fleet Science Center features a variety of nature- and science-themed movies projected onto the 76-foot (23m) tilted-dome screen (shows are daily, with evening screenings on Fri). *Balboa Park (adjacent to Park Blvd.).* ☎ *619/238-1233. www.rhfleet.org. Tickets $12–$20. Bus: 7. Map p 125.*

★★ Landmark Theatres HILL-
CREST/LA JOLLA Indie and foreign films play at these multiscreen (five at Hillcrest, four at La Jolla) cinemas. *Hillcrest Cinema, 3965 Fifth Ave. (btw. University Ave. and Washington St.). Bus: 1, 3, 10, 11, 83, or 120. La Jolla Village, 8879 Villa La Jolla Dr. (at Nobel Dr.). Bus: 30 or 201/202.* ☎ *619/ 819-0236. www.landmarktheatres. com. Tickets $8–$11. Map p 125.*

Opera
★★★ San Diego Opera DOWN-
TOWN A season of both well-trod

The San Diego Opera, downtown.

Sure Bets

San Diego has 18 Native American tribes, half of which operate casinos. The most accessible from downtown is Viejas Casino (5000 Willows Rd., Alpine; ☎ 800/847-6537 or 619/445-5400; www.viejas.com)—it's a straight shot out I-8 (exit Willows Rd.), less than a half-hour's drive away. Viejas also has an outlet center with more than 40 brand-name retailers. Barona Valley Ranch Resort & Casino (1932 Wildcat Canyon Rd., Lakeside; ☎ 888/722-7662 or 619/443-2300; www.barona.com) has 2,000 Vegas-style slots, 70 table games, and an off-track betting area. The resort includes 400 guest rooms, a spa, and an 18-hole championship golf course. Take I-8 east to Hwy. 67 north; at Willows Road, turn right and continue to Wildcat Canyon Road; turn left, and continue 6 miles (10km) to the reservation (allow 40 min. from downtown). Sycuan Resort & Casino is outside El Cajon, at 5469 Casino Way (☎ 800/279-2826 or 619/445-6002; www.sycuan.com). Follow I-8 east for 10 miles (16km) to the El Cajon Boulevard exit. Take El Cajon 3 blocks to Washington Avenue, turning right and continuing on Washington as it turns into Dehesa Road. Stay on Dehesa for 5 miles (8km), and follow the signs (allow 30 min. from downtown). Sycuan features 2,000 slots, 60 game tables, a 1,200-seat bingo palace, and a 450-seat theater that features name touring acts; Sycuan's 54 holes of golf are also some of San Diego's best.

war horses and edgier works runs from late January to mid-May, performed at the Civic Theatre by name talent from around the world, as

San Diego Chargers.

well as local singers. *1200 Third Ave. (at B St.).* ☎ *619/533-7000 (box office) or* ☎ *619/232-7636 (admin). www.sdopera.com. Tickets $30–$210. Bus: Numerous Broadway routes. Trolley: Blue or Orange Line to Civic Center. Map p 125.*

Spectator Sports
★★★ Del Mar Races DEL MAR Thoroughbred racing takes place at the Del Mar Race Track from mid-July to early September. Party crowds come for post-race concerts and other special events; there's year-round satellite wagering at the fairgrounds' Surfside Race Place (☎ 858/755-1167; www.surfsideraceplace.com). *2260 Jimmy Durante Blvd. (at Via de la Valle).* ☎ *858/755-1141. www.dmtc.com. Tickets $5–$15. Bus: 101. Map p 125.*

★★ San Diego Chargers MISSION VALLEY   The city's NFL team plays at Qualcomm Stadium; the season runs from August to December. *9449 Friars Rd. (btw. the 805 and 15 freeways).* ☎ *800/745-3000 or 877/242-7437. www.chargers. com. Tickets $54–$98. Trolley: Green Line or special event Blue Line to Qualcomm Stadium. Map p 125.*

★★★ kids San Diego Padres EAST VILLAGE   Major League Baseball action at PETCO Park, an architecturally striking downtown facility; season runs April to September. *100 Park Blvd. (bordered by Seventh and 10th aves. at J St.).* ☎ *877/374-2784 or 619/795-5000. www.padres.com. Tickets $5–$63. Trolley: Orange or special event line to Gaslamp Quarter; Blue or Orange Line to 12th & Imperial Transit Center or Park & Market. Map p 125.*

★★ San Diego Sockers DEL MAR   San Diego's most successful sports franchise (11 championships) is part of the Professional Arena Soccer League; the season is November to February. *2260 Jimmy Durante Blvd. (at Via de la Valle).* ☎ *866/799-4625. www.sdsockers. com. Tickets $11–$20. Bus: 101.*

PETCO Park in Downtown's East Village.

Diversionary Theatre.

Theater

★★ Diversionary Theatre UNIVERSITY HEIGHTS   This 104-seat theater focuses on plays with gay and lesbian themes. *4545 Park Blvd. (btw. Madison and Monroe aves.).* ☎ *619/220-0097. www.diversionary. org. Tickets $29–$33, $10 student rush 1 hr. prior to curtain. Bus: 11. Map p 125.*

★★★ La Jolla Playhouse LA JOLLA   The Tony Award–winning Playhouse is known for its contemporary takes on classics and commitment to *commedia dell'arte*

Lamb's Players.

both premieres and classics, keeping things on the safe, noncontroversial side. *1142 Orange Ave. (at C Ave.).* ☎ *619/437-0600. www.lambs players.org. Tickets $26–$58. Bus: 901 or 904. Map p 125.*

★★★ The Old Globe Theatre

BALBOA PARK   This Tony Award–winning, three-theater complex attracts big-name playwrights and performers, and has spawned a number of Broadway hits. The summer Shakespeare Festival features three works by the Bard. *Balboa Park (behind the Museum of Man).* ☎ *619/234-5623. www.theoldglobe. org. Tickets $39–$85. Bus: 3, 7, or 120. Map p 125.*

style, as well as for producing Broadway-bound blockbusters. *2910 La Jolla Village Dr. (at Torrey Pines Rd.).* ☎ *858/550-1010. www. lajollaplayhouse.org. Tickets $25–$75. Bus: 30, 41, 101, 150, or 921. Map p 125.*

★★ Lamb's Players Theatre

CORONADO   Featuring a true resident ensemble, Lamb's presents

★★ San Diego Repertory Theatre

GASLAMP QUARTER   The Rep mounts plays and musicals with a strong multicultural bent, performing in the two-stage Lyceum Theatre at Horton Plaza. *79 Broadway Circle, in Horton Plaza.* ☎ *619/544-1000. www.sdrep.org. Tickets $25–$53. Bus: All Broadway routes. Trolley: Civic Center. Map p 125.* ●

Lowell Davies Festival Theater, part of the Old Globe Theatre complex.

Lodging Best Bets

Best **Historic Hotel**
★★★ Hotel Del Coronado $$$$
1500 Orange Ave. (p 139)

Best for a **Romantic Getaway**
★★★ The Lodge at Torrey Pines
$$$$ *11480 N. Torrey Pines Rd.
(p 141)*

Best for **Families**
★★ Paradise Point Resort & Spa
$$$ *1404 Vacation Rd. (p 142)*

Best **Moderately Priced Hotel**
★ Horton Grand Hotel $$ *311
Island Ave. (p 139)*

Best **Budget Hotel**
★★ La Pensione Hotel $ *606 W.
Date St. (p 140)*

Best **Bed & Breakfast**
★★★ Britt Scripps Inn $$$$ *406
Maple St. (p 136)*

Best **Boutique Inn**
★★★ Hotel Parisi $$$$ *1111 Prospect St. (p 139)*

Best **Place to Stay
on the Beach**
★★ Tower 23 $$$$ *723 Felspar St.
(p 143)*

Best **Place to Stay over the
Beach**
★★ Crystal Pier Hotel $$$ *4500
Ocean Blvd. (p 137)*

Best **Green Hotel**
★★ Hotel Indigo $$$ *509 Ninth
Ave. (p 139)*

Best **Place to Watch a Concert
from Your Room**
★★ Hard Rock Hotel San Diego
$$$ *207 Fifth Ave. (p 138)*

Best **Pool**
★★★ Andaz Hotel $$$$ *650 F St.
(p 136)*

Best **Golf Resort**
★★★ Park Hyatt Aviara Resort
$$$$ *7100 Four Seasons Point (p 142)*

Best **Place to Adjust Your
Chakras**
★★ La Costa Resort and Spa $$$$
2100 Costa del Mar Rd. (p 140)

Best for **Baseball Fans**
★★ Omni San Diego Hotel $$$$
675 L St. (p 142)

Best for **Modernists**
★★ Keating Hotel $$$$ *432 F St.
(p 140)*

Best for **Traditionalists**
★★ The Westgate Hotel $$$$
1055 Second Ave. (p 144)

Best **Place to Get Away from
It All**
★★ Loews Coronado Bay Resort
$$$$ *4000 Coronado Bay Rd. (p 141)*

Park Hyatt Aviara Resort.

Previous page: The pool at Paradise Point.

Downtown Hotels

Andaz Hotel **11**
Best Western Bayside Inn **4**
Britt Scripps Inn **1**
Gaslamp Plaza Suites **9**
Hard Rock Hotel San Diego **16**
Hilton San Diego Gaslamp Quarter **17**
Holiday Inn on the Bay **3**
Horton Grand **18**
Hotel Indigo **12**
Hotel Solamar **13**
Keating Hotel **10**
La Pensione Hotel **2**
Manchester Grand Hyatt San Diego **20**
Marriott San Diego Gaslamp Quarter **14**
Marriott San Diego Hotel & Marina **19**
Omni San Diego Hotel **15**
Sè San Diego **8**
The US Grant **7**
W San Diego **5**
The Westgate Hotel **6**

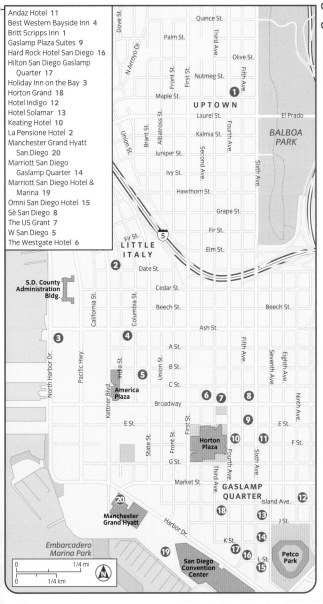

Mission Bay Hotels

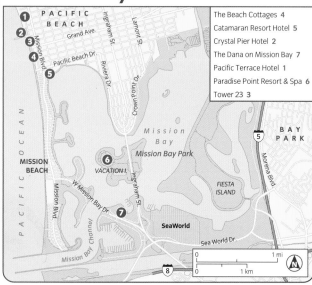

The Beach Cottages 4
Catamaran Resort Hotel 5
Crystal Pier Hotel 2
The Dana on Mission Bay 7
Pacific Terrace Hotel 1
Paradise Point Resort & Spa 6
Tower 23 3

La Jolla Hotels

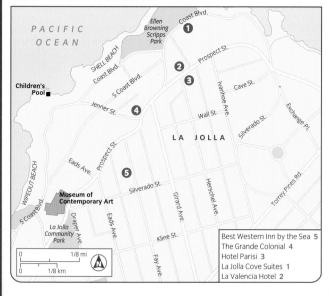

Best Western Inn by the Sea 5
The Grande Colonial 4
Hotel Parisi 3
La Jolla Cove Suites 1
La Valencia Hotel 2

Beach Hotels

Balboa Park Inn 11
Coronado Inn 13
Del Mar Motel on the Beach 3
El Cordova Hotel 14
Estancia La Jolla Hotel and Spa 9
Glorietta Bay Inn 15
The Grand Del Mar 7
Hotel del Coronado 16
La Costa Resort and Spa 2
La Jolla Shores Hotel 10
L'Auberge Del Mar Resort & Spa 4
Les Artistes 6
The Lodge at Torrey Pines 8
Loews Coronado Bay Resort 17
Park Hyatt Aviara Resort 1
Park Manor Suites 12
Wave Crest 5

Lodging **A to Z**

Rooftop pool at the Andaz.

★★★ Andaz Hotel GASLAMP QUARTER A dowdy old hotel has been magically transformed into a world-class, high-style luxury destination. It features a multilevel nightclub and rooftop pool/entertainment area. *600 F St. (btw. Sixth and Seventh aves.).* ☎ *877/489-4489. www. andazsandiego.com. 159 units. Doubles from $199. AE, DC, DISC, MC, V. Bus: 3 or 120. Map p 133.*

★ Balboa Park Inn HILLCREST Popular with gay travelers, the hotel features specialty accommodations with fanciful themes, from Art Deco to Orient Express. *3402 Park Blvd. (at Upas St.).* ☎ *800/938-8181. www.balboaparkinn.com. 26 units. Doubles $99 w/breakfast. AE, DC, DISC, MC, V. Bus: 7. Map p 135.*

The Beach Cottages PACIFIC BEACH This family-owned operation has been around since 1948 and offers a variety of guest quarters, including cottages just steps from the sand. *4255 Ocean Blvd. (1 block south of Grand Ave.).* ☎ *858/483-7440. www.beachcottages.com. 61 units. Doubles from $140. AE, DC, DISC, MC, V. Bus: 8/9 or 30. Map p 134.*

Best Western Bayside Inn DOWNTOWN Accommodations here are basic chain-hotel issue, but they are well maintained and have balconies overlooking the bay or downtown. *555 W. Ash St. (at Columbia St.).* ☎ *800/341-1818. www.bay sideinn.com. 122 units. Doubles $189 w/breakfast. AE, DC, DISC, MC, V. Bus: 83. Trolley: Blue or Orange Line to America Plaza. Map p 133.*

★ Best Western Inn by the Sea LA JOLLA Occupying an enviable location in the heart of La Jolla's charming village, this property is just a short walk from the cliffs and beach. *7830 Fay Ave. (btw. Prospect and Silverado sts.).* ☎ *800/526-4545. www.bestwestern.com/innbythesea. 129 units. Doubles from $159 w/ breakfast. AE, DC, DISC, MC, V. Bus: 30. Map p 134.*

★★★ Britt Scripps Inn BANKERS HILL A glorious Victorian house lovingly converted into an intimate "estate hotel"—part B&B, part luxury hotel. *406 Maple St. (at Fourth Ave.).* ☎ *888/881-1991. www.britt scripps.com. 9 units. Doubles from $399 w/breakfast and afternoon wine and hors d'oeuvres. AE, DC, MC, V. Bus: 3 or 120. Map p 133.*

★★ kids Catamaran Resort Hotel PACIFIC BEACH Right on Mission Bay, this Polynesian-themed resort has its own beach, complete with watersports facilities. *3999 Mission Blvd. (4 blocks south of Grand Ave.).* ☎ *800/422-8386. www. catamaranresort.com. 313 units. Doubles from $274. AE, DC, DISC, MC, V. Bus: 8/9. Map p 134.*

★ Coronado Inn CORONADO This tropically flavored 1940s motel is centrally located and terrifically priced, and maintains a friendly

Britt Scripps Inn.

ambience. *266 Orange Ave. (corner of 3rd St.).* ☎ *800/598-6624. www. coronadoinn.com. 30 units. Doubles from $119 w/breakfast. AE, DISC, MC, V. Bus: 901 or 904. Map p 135.*

★★ kids Crystal Pier Hotel

PACIFIC BEACH   This utterly unique cluster of cottages literally sits over the surf on the vintage Crystal Pier. *4500 Ocean Blvd. (at Garnet Ave.).* ☎ *800/748-5894. www.crystalpier. com. 29 units. Doubles from $300. DISC, MC, V. Bus: 8/9, 27, or 30. Map p 134.*

★ The Dana on Mission Bay

MISSION BAY   Some rooms here overlook bobbing sailboats on the recreational marina; beaches and SeaWorld are a 15-minute walk away. *1710 W. Mission Bay Dr. (off Ingraham St.).* ☎ *800/345-9995. www.thedana.com. 271 units. Doubles from $239. AE, DC, DISC, MC, V. Bus: 8/9. Map p 134.*

Del Mar Motel on the Beach

DEL MAR   The only property in Del Mar right on the beach, this simply furnished little white-stucco motel has been here since 1946. *1702 Coast Blvd. (at 17th St.).* ☎ *800/223-8449. www.delmarmotelonthebeach. com. 44 units. Doubles from $259.*

AE, DC, DISC, MC, V. Bus: 101. Map p 135.

★ El Cordova Hotel CORONADO

With its courtyard, meandering pathways, and prime location across from the Hotel del Coronado, this Spanish hacienda is a popular option. *1351 Orange Ave. (at Adella Ave.).* ☎ *800/229-2032. www. elcordovahotel.com. 40 units. Doubles from $225. AE, DC, DISC, MC, V. Bus: 901 or 904. Map p 135.*

★★★ Estancia La Jolla Hotel and Spa LA JOLLA   This romantic,

California rancho-style property features meticulously maintained gardens, an award-winning restaurant, and an indulgent spa. *9700 N. Torrey Pines Rd. (north of Almahurst Row).* ☎ *877/437-8262. www.estanciala jolla.com. 210 units. Doubles from $229. AE, DC, DISC, MC, V. Bus: 101. Map p 135.*

★★ Gaslamp Plaza Suites

GASLAMP QUARTER   At 11 stories, this was San Diego's first skyscraper, built in 1913. Most rooms are spacious and offer luxuries rare in this price range. *520 E St. (corner of Fifth Ave.).* ☎ *800/874-8770. www. gaslampplaza.com. 64 units. Doubles from $119 w/breakfast. AE, DC, DISC, MC, V. Bus: 3, 120, or any Broadway route. Trolley: Blue or Orange Line to Fifth Ave. Map p 133.*

Glorietta Bay Inn.

The Grande Colonial.

★★ Glorietta Bay Inn CORONADO
Across the street from the Hotel del Coronado, this pretty hotel consists of the charmingly historic John D. Spreckels mansion (1908) and several newer, motel-style buildings. *1630 Glorietta Blvd. (near Orange Ave.).* ☎ *800/283-9383. www.gloriettabayinn.com. 100 units. Doubles from $185 w/breakfast. AE, DC, DISC, MC, V. Bus: 901 or 904. Map p 135.*

★★★ The Grande Colonial LA JOLLA
This refined, elegant hotel possesses an old-world European flair that's more London or Georgetown than seaside La Jolla. *910 Prospect St. (btw. Fay and Girard aves.).* ☎ *888/530-5766. www.thegrande colonial.com. 93 units. Doubles from $295. AE, DC, MC, V. Bus: 30. Map p 134.*

★★★ The Grand Del Mar DEL MAR
The name is no idle boast. Resembling a Tuscan villa, this luxury resort has a Vegas-like opulence and incorporates a Tom Fazio–designed golf course and one of San Diego's finest restaurants. *5300 Grand Del Mar Court (off Carmel Country Rd.).* ☎ *888/314-2030. www.thegranddelmar.com. 249 units. Doubles from $390. AE, DC, DISC, MC, V. No public transportation. Map p 135.*

★★ Hard Rock Hotel San Diego GASLAMP QUARTER
This 12-story condo-hotel has a sweet location, a celebrity-chef restaurant, and an outdoor concert space. The Black Eyed Peas designed one of the "Rock Star" suites. *207 Fifth Ave. (btw. K and L sts.).* ☎ *866/751-7625. www.hardrockhotelsd.com. 420 units. Doubles from $319. AE, DC, DISC, MC, V. Trolley: Orange Line to Gaslamp Quarter. Map p 133.*

★★★ Hilton San Diego Gaslamp Quarter GASLAMP QUARTER
This handsome hotel incorporates elements of a historic building. It's also a great place for guests who want to be in the heart of the Gaslamp action. *401 K St. (at Fourth Ave.).* ☎ *800/445-8667. www.hilton.com. 283 units. Doubles from $289. AE, DC, DISC, MC, V. Trolley: Orange Line to Gaslamp Quarter or Convention Center. Map p 133.*

★★ kids Holiday Inn on the Bay EMBARCADERO
This three-building high-rise complex has a scenic location across from the harbor and the Maritime Museum, only 1½ miles (2.4km) from the airport. *1355 N. Harbor Dr. (at Ash St.).* ☎ *800/972-2802. www.holiday-inn.com/san-onthebay. 600 units. Doubles from $185. AE, DC, MC, V. Bus: 2, 210, 810, 820, 850, 860, 923, or*

Grand Del Mar.

Hard Rock Hotel San Diego.

992. Trolley: Blue or Orange Line to America Plaza. Map p 133.

★ **Horton Grand** GASLAMP QUARTER   The charming Horton Grand combines two hotels built in 1886. Both were saved from demolition and moved to this spot. *311 Island Ave. (at Fourth Ave.).* ☎ *800/ 542-1886. www.hortongrand.com. 132 units. Doubles from $179. AE, DC, MC, V. Bus: 3, 11, or 120. Trolley: Orange Line to Convention Center. Map p 133.*

★★★ **Hotel del Coronado** CORONADO   Opened in 1888 and designated a National Historic Landmark in 1977, the Hotel Del is the last of California's stately old seaside hotels and a monument to Victorian grandeur. *1500 Orange Ave. (at Dana Place).* ☎ *800/468-3533. www.hoteldel.com. 757 rooms. Doubles from $425. AE, DC, DISC, MC, V. Bus: 901 or 904. Map p 135.*

★★ **Hotel Indigo** EAST VILLAGE Green is the primary color at this new boutique property—it's San Diego's first LEED-certified hotel. The state-of-the-art rooms have a livable, residential feel and don't scrimp on comfort. *509 Ninth Ave. (at Island Ave.).* ☎ *877/846-3446. www.hotelindigo.com/sandiego. 210 units. Doubles from $225. AE, DC,*

DISC, MC, V. Bus: 3, 11, 901, or 929. Map p 133.

★★★ **Hotel Parisi** LA JOLLA Feng shui principles and outstanding service hold sway at this boutique hotel; the Italy-meets-Zen composition is carried into the spacious rooms, where custom furnishings are modern yet comfy. *1111 Prospect St. (at Herschel Ave.).* ☎ *877/472-7474. www.hotelparisi. com. 29 units. Doubles from $295 w/ breakfast. AE, DC, DISC, MC, V. Bus: 30. Map p 134.*

★★ **Hotel Solamar** GASLAMP QUARTER   This stylishly urban and sophisticated property provides excellent Gaslamp digs. The fourth-floor pool bar is a hot spot. *435 Sixth Ave. (btw. J St. and Island*

Hotel Solamar.

Keating Hotel.

Ave.). ☎ 877/230-0300. www.hotel solamar.com. 235 units. Doubles from $189. AE, DC, DISC, MC, V. Bus: 3 or 120. Trolley: Orange Line to Gaslamp Quarter. Map p 133.

★★ **Keating Hotel** GASLAMP QUARTER The Italian design group behind Ferrari and Maserati made its first foray into hotel design with this ultra-contemporary project, set in a gorgeous structure built in 1890. 432 F St. (btw. Fourth and Fifth aves.). ☎ 877/753-2846. www.keatinghotel. com. 35 units. Doubles from $249. AE, DC, DISC, MC, V. Bus: 3, 120, or 992. Map p 133.

★★★ **L'Auberge Del Mar Resort & Spa** DEL MAR An excellent spa and one of the area's finest restaurants highlight this

L'Auberge del Mar.

elegant hotel, across from Del Mar's shopping and dining scene, and a short walk (down a private path) from the beach. 1540 Camino del Mar (at 15th St.). ☎ 800/245-9757. www.laubergedelmar.com. 120 units. Doubles from $350. AE, DC, MC, V. Bus: 101. Map p 135.

★★ **kids La Costa Resort and Spa** CARLSBAD This campus-like golf and tennis resort has a California mission style. There's also a 42-room spa and the new-age Chopra Center for adults, waterslides and entertainment for the kids. 2100 Costa del Mar Rd. (at El Camino Real). ☎ 800/854-5000. www. lacosta.com. 610 units. Doubles from $279. AE, DC, DISC, MC, V. Bus: 309. Map p 135.

La Jolla Cove Suites LA JOLLA Across from Ellen Browning Scripps Park, this family-run 1950s-era hotel has to-die-for ocean views and is steps away from the Cove. 1155 Coast Blvd. (across from La Jolla Cove). ☎ 888/525-6552. www.la jollacove.com. 113 units. Doubles from $242 w/breakfast. AE, DC, DISC, MC, V. Bus: 30. Map p 134.

★ **kids La Jolla Shores Hotel** LA JOLLA Spend time on the beach or the tennis courts at this three-story 1960s hotel in a mainly residential enclave. 8110 Camino del Oro (at Avenida de la Playa). ☎ 866/392-8762. www.ljshoreshotel.com. 128 units. Doubles from $359. AE, DC, DISC, MC, V. Bus: 30. Map p 135.

★★ **La Pensione Hotel** LITTLE ITALY This place has a lot going for it: modern amenities, remarkable value, a convenient location, a friendly staff, and free parking. 606 W. Date St. (at India St.). ☎ 800/ 232-4683. www.lapensionehotel. com. 75 units. Doubles $80. AE, DC, DISC, MC, V. Bus: 83. Trolley: Blue Line to County Center/Little Italy. Map p 133.

★★★ La Valencia Hotel LA
JOLLA This blufftop hotel, which looks like a Mediterranean villa, has been the centerpiece of La Jolla since opening in 1926; La V's clubby Whaling Bar is a classic. *1132 Prospect St. (at Herschel Ave.).* ☎ *800/451-0772. www.lavalencia. com. 113 units. Doubles from $299. AE, DC, DISC, MC, V. Bus: 30. Map p 134.*

Les Artistes DEL MAR A funky,
informal hotel, just a few blocks from downtown Del Mar, where the rooms have been redone as tributes to favored artists like Diego Rivera. *944 Camino del Mar (btw. Ninth and 10th sts.).* ☎ *858/755-4646. www. lesartistesinn.com. 12 units. Doubles from $105 w/breakfast. DISC, MC, V. Bus: 101. Map p 135.*

★★★ The Lodge at Torrey
Pines LA JOLLA This AAA 5- Diamond resort is a Craftsman-style fantasy brimming with clinker-brick masonry, Stickley furniture, and exquisite pottery. Some rooms overlook the golf course and the ocean. *11480 N. Torrey Pines Rd. (at Callan Rd.).* ☎ *800/656-0087. www. lodgetorreypines.com. 171 units. Doubles from $375. AE, DC, DISC, MC, V. Bus: 101. Map p 135.*

La Costa.

★★ kids Loews Coronado Bay
Resort CORONADO Located on its own private peninsula 4 miles (6.5km) south of downtown Coronado, this isolated resort destination has a plethora of water-related activities. *4000 Coronado Bay Rd. (off Silver Strand Blvd.).* ☎ *866/563-9792. www.loewshotels.com. 439 units. Doubles from $240. AE, DC, DISC, MC, V. Bus: 901. Map p 135.*

★ Manchester Grand Hyatt
San Diego EMBARCADERO This twin-towered behemoth is adjacent to the Convention Center and Seaport Village shopping center, creating a neatly insular, if touristy, little world. *1 Market Place (Market St. at*

Courtyard at La Valencia Hotel.

The Lodge at Torrey Pines.

Harbor Dr.). ☎ 800/233-1234. www.
manchestergrand.hyatt.com. 1,625
units. Doubles from $269. AE, DC,
DISC, MC, V. Trolley: Orange Line to
Seaport Village. Map p 133.

★ **Marriott San Diego
Gaslamp Quarter** GASLAMP
QUARTER A massive renovation
transformed this property into a
stylish destination with a boutique
feel. Check out the open-air bar on
the 22nd floor. 660 K St. (btw. Sixth
and Seventh aves.). ☎ 888/800-
8118. www.sandiegogaslamphotel.
com. 306 units. Doubles from $279.
AE, DC, DISC, MC, V. Trolley: Orange
Line to Gaslamp Quarter. Map p 133.

Manchester Grand Hyatt.

★★ **Marriott San Diego Hotel
& Marina** EMBARCADERO Con-
ventiongoers are drawn to the scenic 446-slip marina, lush grounds,
waterfall pool, and breathtaking
bay-and-beyond views. 333 W. Harbor Dr. (at Front St.). ☎ 800/228-
9290. www.marriott.com. 1,362
units. Doubles from $335. AE, DC,
DISC, MC, V. Trolley: Orange Line to
Convention Center. Map p 133.

★★ **Omni San Diego Hotel**
GASLAMP QUARTER This swank
32-story high-rise has lots of baseball memorabilia and a fourth-floor
"skybridge" that connects it with
PETCO Park—it's baseball fan
heaven. 675 L St. (at Sixth Ave.).
☎ 888/444-6664. www.omnihotels.
com. 511 units. Doubles from $329.
AE, DC, DISC, MC, V. Trolley: Orange
Line to Gaslamp Quarter. Map p 133.

★ **Pacific Terrace Hotel** PACIFIC
BEACH More upscale than most of
the casual places nearby, this
boardwalk hotel features a South
Seas–meets–Spanish Colonial ambience. 610 Diamond St. (west of Mission Blvd.). ☎ 800/344-3370. www.
pacificterrace.com. 73 units. Doubles
from $359. AE, DC, DISC, MC, V. Bus:
30. Map p 134.

★★ kids **Paradise Point Resort
& Spa** MISSION BAY Smack-dab
in the middle of Mission Bay, this
hotel complex is almost as much a
theme park as its closest neighbor,
SeaWorld (a 3-min. drive away).
1404 Vacation Rd. (off Ingraham St.).
☎ 800/344-2626. www.paradise
point.com. 462 units. Doubles from
$329. AE, DC, DISC, MC, V. Bus: 8/9.
Map p 134.

★★★ kids **Park Hyatt Aviara
Resort** CARLSBAD This oceanview property is no longer a Four
Seasons, but it's still a sumptuous
resort with an outstanding spa,

Siren Pool and Uber Lounge, Sè San Diego.

restaurant, golf course, and activities for the kids. *7100 Four Seasons Point (at Aviara Pkwy.).* ☎ 760/448-1234. www.parkaviara.hyatt.com. *329 units. Doubles from $280. AE, DC, DISC, MC, V. No public transportation. Map p 135.*

★ **Park Manor Suites** HILLCREST This eight-story property, built in 1926, occupies a prime corner overlooking Balboa Park; a few rooms have glassed-in terraces. *525 Spruce St. (btw. Fifth and Sixth aves.).* ☎ 800/874-2649. www.parkmanor suites.com. *74 units. Doubles from $169 w/breakfast. AE, DC, DISC, MC, V. Bus: 3 or 120. Map p 135.*

★★ **Sè San Diego** DOWNTOWN This sexy hotel features an Asian-chic vibe and a happening pool lounge where the beautiful people come to party. *1047 Fifth Ave. (at Broadway).* ☎ 877/515-2211. www.sesandiego.com. *184 units. Doubles from $229. AE, DISC, MC, V. Bus: 3, 120, or numerous Broadway routes. Trolley: Fifth Ave. Map p 133.*

★★ **Tower 23** PACIFIC BEACH This modernist beach resort sits right alongside the boardwalk in Pacific Beach. *723 Felspar St. (west of Mission Blvd.).* ☎ 866/869-3723. www.t23hotel.com. *44 units. Doubles from $309. AE, DC, MC, V. Bus: 8/9, 27, or 30. Map p 134.*

★★★ **The US Grant** DOWNTOWN Built in 1910, this grandiose 11-story property is a Beaux Arts beauty and

Tower 23.

Downtown's historic U.S. Grant.

one of San Diego's most historic hotels. The clubby Grant Grill has long been a spot for power lunches and dinners. *326 Broadway (btw. Third and Fourth aves., main entrance on Fourth Ave.).* ☎ *800/ 237-5029. www.usgrant.net. 270 units. Doubles from $309. AE, DC, DISC, MC, V. Bus: 2, 3, 120, 992, or all Broadway routes. Trolley: Orange or Blue Line to Civic Center. Map p 133.*

W San Diego.

★★ **W San Diego** DOWNTOWN There's an adventurous restaurant, lively nightspots, and accommodations that are bright and cheery— like mod beach cabanas. *421 W. B St. (at State St.).* ☎ *619/398-3100. www.whotels.com/sandiego. 259 units. Doubles from $270. AE, DC, DISC, MC, V. Bus: All Broadway routes. Trolley: Blue or Orange Line to America Plaza. Map p 133.*

★★ **Wave Crest** DEL MAR On a bluff overlooking the Pacific, these gray-shingled bungalow condominiums are beautifully maintained and wonderfully private. *1400 Ocean Ave. (south of 15th St.).* ☎ *858/755- 0100. www.wavecrestresort.com. 31 units. Studios from $220. MC, V. Bus: 101. Map p 135.*

★★ **The Westgate Hotel** DOWN-TOWN With its regal and lavish decor, this is about as "old world" as San Diego gets. It's a hub of cultural and culinary activities, as well. *1055 Second Ave. (btw. Broadway and C St.).* ☎ *800/522-1564. www. westgatehotel.com. 223 units. Doubles from $370. AE, DC, DISC, MC, V. Bus: 2, 7, 923, 929, or all Broadway routes. Trolley: Blue or Orange Line to Civic Center. Map p 133.* ●

North County

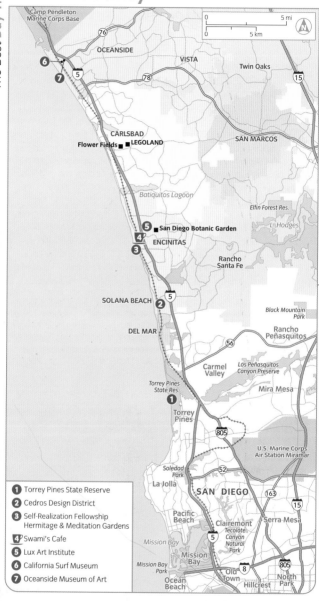

Flower Fields ■ ■ LEGOLAND

■ San Diego Botanic Garden

1. Torrey Pines State Reserve
2. Cedros Design District
3. Self-Realization Fellowship Hermitage & Meditation Gardens
4. Swami's Cafe
5. Lux Art Institute
6. California Surf Museum
7. Oceanside Museum of Art

Previous page: The Anza Borrego Desert.

Don't be fooled by the laid-back, surf-dude ethic that prevails among the string of picturesque coastal communities north of La Jolla. For decades, the area's slower pace and stunning physical beauty have attracted artists, writers, celebrities, spiritualists, and others who could afford a piece of coastal solitude. The result is a casual sophistication and territorial pride that distinguishes this region from the county's lower reaches. START: **Del Mar is 18 miles (29km) north of downtown San Diego, Carlsbad about 33 miles (53km), and Oceanside approximately 36 miles (58km). If you're driving, follow I-5 north; Del Mar, Solana Beach, Encinitas, Carlsbad, and Oceanside all have freeway exits. The northernmost point, Oceanside, will take about 45 minutes. The other choice by car is to wander up the old coast road, known as Camino del Mar, "PCH" (Pacific Coast Highway), Old Highway 101, and County Highway S21. The Breeze 101 bus route traverses 101 from La Jolla to Oceanside. From San Diego, the Coaster commuter train provides service to Solana Beach, Encinitas, Carlsbad, and Oceanside, and Amtrak stops in Solana Beach and Oceanside. The Coaster makes the trip a number of times (6:30am–7pm) on weekdays, four times on Saturday; Amtrak passes through about 11 times daily each way. For the Coaster, call ☎ 800/262-7837 or 511, or visit www. transit.511sd.com; check with Amtrak at ☎ 800/872-7245 or www. amtrak.com. If you are driving, beware of rush-hour traffic.**

① ★★★ **Torrey Pines State Reserve.** Simply one of the most breathtaking locations in San Diego County, this park is home to the gnarled little tree that's the rarest native tree in North America. *See p 97, bullet* ①.

② ★★★ **Cedros Design District.** This vivacious neighborhood is loaded with home decor and clothing boutiques, art galleries, and cafes. ⏲ *At least 1 hr. See p 78.*

③ ★★ **Self-Realization Fellowship Hermitage and Meditation Gardens.** Paramahansa Yogananda, a guru born and educated in India, opened this retreat with the exotic lotus domes in 1937. He lived for many years in the Hermitage, and today the site serves as a spiritual sanctuary for his followers.

The serene meditation gardens offer spectacular ocean views and are a terrific place to cool off on a hot day (and no disciples will give you a sales pitch). ⏲ *30 min. 215 W. K St. (off S. Coast Hwy. 101).* ☎ *760/753-2888. www.yogananda-srf.org. Free admission. Tues–Sat 9am–5pm; Sun 11am–5pm (Hermitage open Sun 2–5pm).*

Torrey Pines State Reserve.

Grape Escape

Over the line in Riverside County, 60 miles (97km) north of San Diego via I-15, is the wine country of Temecula (pronounced "ta-*meck*-you-la"). Some believe Franciscan friars planted the first grapevines here in the early 1800s, and there are now 25-plus wineries in the region (most are along Rancho California Road). Harvest time is generally from mid-August to September, but visitors are invited year-round to tour, taste, and stock up. For more information contact the Temecula Valley Winegrowers Association (☎ 800/801-9463; www.temeculawines.org) or the Temecula Valley Convention and Visitors Bureau (☎ 888/363-2852; www.temecula cvb.com), which can provide information on accommodations, golf, fishing, and the Temecula Valley Balloon & Wine Festival, held in June. Grapeline (☎ 888/894-6379; www.gogrape.com) can pick you up from your hotel and shuttle you on a wine country tour.

Locals crowd into the casual and inexpensive **4** ★ **Swami's Cafe** for tasty, health-conscious breakfasts and lunch. It gets its name from the legendary surf spot across the highway, which in turn was named for the yogi's retreat on the clifftop. *1163 S. Coast Hwy. 101 (at W. K St.).* ☎ *760/944-0612. www.swamis. signonsandiego.com. Daily 7am–4pm. $5–$9.*

5 ★★ **Lux Art Institute.** This unique facility allows visitors to watch as an artist in residence paints, sculpts, or draws in a studio environment. The building itself is a work of art. ⏱ *45 min. 1550 S. El Camino Real (north of Manchester Ave.).* ☎ *760/436-6611. www.luxart institute.com. Admission $10 adults (good for 2 visits), free for ages 20 and under. Thurs–Fri 1–5pm; Sat 11am–5pm.*

Meditation Gardens at the Self-Realization Fellowship.

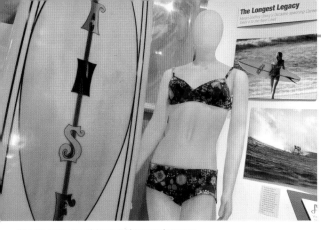

Women on Waves *exhibit at California Surf Museum.*

6 ★ kids California Surf Museum. This slick, oceanfront facility opened in 2009 and features an extensive collection documenting the early days of surfing. The gift shop sells surf-themed goods. ⏱ *45 min. 312 Pier View Way (at N. Cleveland St.).* ☎ *760/721-6876. www.surfmuseum.org. Admission $3 adults, $1 seniors and students, free for kids 11 and under. Daily 10am–4pm.*

7 ★★ Oceanside Museum of Art. Cutting-edge and classic California Deco architecture cozy up together at this beautiful museum presenting contemporary artwork by both regional and international artists. ⏱ *45 min. 704 Pier View Way (at N. Ditmar St.).* ☎ *760/435-3720. www.oma-online.org. Admission $8 adults, $5 seniors, free for students and military. Tues–Sat 10am–4pm; Sun 1–4pm.*

Flower Power

San Diego's North County is a noted flower-growing region, and there are two places that will be of special interest to the horticulturally minded: the ★ San Diego Botanic Garden in Encinitas and the ★ Flower Fields at Carlsbad. The serene Botanic Garden, 230 Quail Gardens Dr. (☎ 760/436-3036; www.sdbgarden.com), boasts the country's largest bamboo collection, plus some 35 acres (14 hectares) of native and exotic flora. The Flower Fields, 5704 Paseo del Norte (☎ 760/431-0352; www.theflowerfields.com), is a working nursery where a spectacular sea of ranunculus blossom every March to mid-May. Visitors can tour the grounds and enjoy a number of special floral installations.

Flower Fields at Carlsbad.

Julian

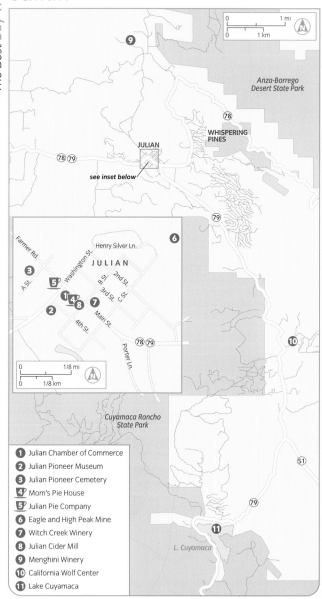

1 mi
1 km

Anza-Borrego Desert State Park

78 79

JULIAN

78

WHISPERING PINES

79

see inset below

Farmer Rd.

Henry Silver Ln.

6

JULIAN

3

5

2nd St.

B St.

3rd St.

2

C St.

1 4 8

7

Main St.

4th St.

Porter Ln.

78 79

0   1/8 mi
0   1/8 km

10

Cuyamaca Rancho State Park

51

79

11

L. Cuyamaca

1 Julian Chamber of Commerce
2 Julian Pioneer Museum
3 Julian Pioneer Cemetery
4 Mom's Pie House
5 Julian Pie Company
6 Eagle and High Peak Mine
7 Witch Creek Winery
8 Julian Cider Mill
9 Menghini Winery
10 California Wolf Center
11 Lake Cuyamaca

A trip to Julian is a taste of the Old West. Prospectors first ventured into these fertile hills (elevation 4,225 ft./1,288m) in search of gold in the late 1860s, and within 10 years, 18 mines were operating, producing up to an estimated $13 million worth of gold. After the rush played out, this quaint Victorian town (pop. 3,000) found fame thanks to another mother lode: apples. START: **Julian is not accessible via public transportation. You can make the 90-minute drive on Hwy. 78 or I-8 to Hwy. 79; try taking one route going and the other on the way back (Hwy. 79 winds through Rancho Cuyamaca State Park, while Hwy. 78 traverses open country and farmland). Weekend crowds can be heavy, especially during the fall apple-harvest season. Fall temperatures are brisk; snow is possible in winter.**

❶ Julian Chamber of Commerce. Staffers at the Chamber of Commerce, located in the foyer of the creaky old Town Hall (built in 1913), always have enthusiastic suggestions for local activities. Be sure to duck into the auditorium itself to check out the photos of Julian's bygone days. Main Street is only 6 blocks long, and shops, cafes, and some lodgings are on it or a block away—town maps and accommodations fliers are available on the Town Hall porch. Public restrooms are behind the building. *2129 Main St. (at Washington St.).* ☎ *760/765-1857. www.julianca.com. Daily 10am–4pm.*

❷ Julian Pioneer Museum. This small museum is dedicated to illuminating the life and times of Julian's townspeople from 1869–1913. It displays clothing, tools, gold-mining equipment, household and military items, and a fine collection of lace doilies, quilts, and scarves. Look out back for the Julian Transportation Garage museum, with its vintage machinery and vehicles. 🕐 *30 min. 2811 Washington St. (south of Fourth St.).* ☎ *760/765-0227. $3 donation requested. Apr–Nov Tues–Sun 10am–4pm; weekends 10am–4pm the rest of the year.*

A horse-drawn carriage in the streets of Julian.

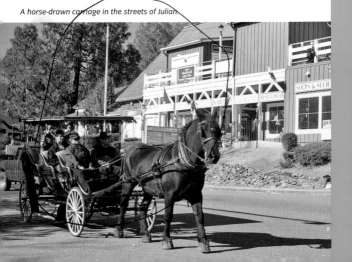

The Julian Pioneer Museum.

❸ ★ Julian Pioneer Cemetery.
This small, hillside graveyard is straight out of *Our Town*. Julian's citizenry have been laid to rest here since 1870, when the only way to deliver caskets to the gravesite was to carry them up the long, stone staircase in front. If you don't want to huff and puff up the stairs (just imagine carrying a casket), there's now a parking lot behind the cemetery that provides easy access.
🕐 *20 min. A St. (at Farmer Rd).*

You've waited long enough—it's time for some pie. You can observe the mom-on-duty rolling crust and

You're never far from first-rate apple pie in Julian.

crimping edges at **❹ ★★ Mom's Pie House** (2119 Main St.; ☎ 760/765-2472; www.momspiesjulian.com; $5–$16). The shop routinely bakes several varieties of apple pie as well as seasonal specialties. Lunch is served weekdays (11am–3pm) and some weekends. Mon–Fri 8am–5pm; weekends 8am–6pm.

Enjoy the outdoor seating at **❺ ★★ Julian Pie Company** (2225 Main St.; ☎ 760/765-2449; www.julianpie.com; $5–$16), where overhanging apples are literally up for grabs. Among its specialties is a no-sugar-added pie; light lunches of soup and sandwiches are offered weekdays (11am–2pm). Daily 9am–5pm.

❻ ★ kids Eagle and High Peak Mine. Although seemingly a tourist trap, this mine, which dates from around 1870, offers an interesting and educational look at the town's one-time economic mainstay. Tours take you underground to the 1,000-foot (305m) hard-rock tunnel to see the mining and milling process; antique engines and authentic tools are on display. 🕐 *1 hr. End of C St. (at Old Miner's Trail).* ☎ 760/765-0036. $10 adults, $5 children 6–11,

$1 for children 5 and under. Hour-long tours are usually given beginning at 10am, but hours vary so it's best to call ahead.

7 Witch Creek Winery. There are a handful of wineries in the Julian area, but this is the only wine-tasting operation right in town. What it lacks in ambience, it makes up for in convenience and friendliness. ⊙ *30 min. 2100 Main St. (btw. B and C sts.).* ☎ *760/765-2023. www.witchcreekwinery.com. Daily 11am–5pm.*

8 ★★ Julian Cider Mill. You can see cider presses at work here October through March. It offers free tastes of the fresh nectar, and jugs to take home. Throughout the year, the mill also carries the area's widest selection of food products, from apple butters and jams to berry preserves, several varieties of local honey, candies, and other goodies. ⊙ *20 min. 2103 Main St. (at B St.).* ☎ *760/765-1430. Mon–Thurs 9:30am–5pm; Fri–Sun 9:30am–5:30pm.*

9 ★★ Menghini Winery. The rustic facilities and rolling picnic grounds of this winery make it a popular spot not only for wine tasting, but also for special events like the annual Grape Stomp Festa and Menghini Arts and Music Festival in September, and the Apple Days Festival in October. It's located about 3 miles (5km) out of town. ⊙ *1 hr. 1150 Julian Orchards Dr. (at Wynola Rd.).* ☎ *760/765-2072. www.menghiniwinery.com. Mon–Fri 10am–4pm; Sat–Sun 10am–5pm.*

10 ★★ kids California Wolf Center. Animal lovers should look into this education and conservation center, located about 4 miles (6.5km) from town, where you can

Julian's most famous product, fresh from the oven.

learn about wolves and visit with the resident wolf pack. Reservations required. ⊙ *1 hr. 18457 Hwy. 79 (at KQ Ranch Campground, look for Wolf Center sign).* ☎ *760/765-0030. www.californiawolfcenter.org. $10–$20. Sat at 2pm; Sun at 10am; private tours can be arranged Tues–Fri ($25 per person).*

11 ★ kids Lake Cuyamaca. Eight miles (13km) south of Julian this 110-acre (45-hectare) lake offers boating, fishing, and camping. Anglers try for trout (stocked year-round), bass, catfish, crappie, and bluegill. There's also a general store and restaurant at the lake's edge. ⊙ *At least 1 hr. 15027 Hwy. 79 (btw. Milk Ranch and Wolahi roads).* ☎ *877/581-9904. www.lake cuyamaca.org. Fishing fee $6 per day, $3.50 per day for ages 8–15, free for children 7 and under. A California fishing license is required and sold here: $13 for the day. Rowboats $15 per day, motorboats $45 per day ($35 after 1pm), canoes and paddleboats (summer only) $15 per hour. Daily 6am–sunset (weather permitting).*

Tijuana

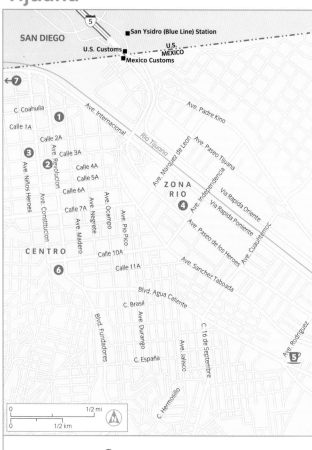

5

SAN DIEGO

■ San Ysidro (Blue Line) Station

U.S. Customs ■

■ U.S.
MEXICO

■ Mexico Customs

← 7

C. Coahuila

1

Calle 1A

Ave. Internacional

Ave. Padre Kino

Rio Tijuana

3

Calle 2A

Calle 3A

Ave. Revolucion

2

Calle 4A

Calle 5A

Calle 6A

Ave. Niños Heroes

Ave. Marquez de Leon

Ave. Paseo Tijuana

**ZONA
RIO**

Ave. Independencia

Via Rapida Oriente

Calle 7A

Ave. Constitucion

Ave. Negrete

Ave. Ocampo

Ave. Pio Pico

4

Via Rapida Poniente

Ave. Cuauhtemoc

Ave. Madero

Calle 10A

Ave. Paseo de los Heroes

CENTRO

6

Calle 11A

Ave. Sanchez Taboada

Blvd. Agua Caliente

C. Brasil

C. España

Blvd. Fundadores

Ave. Durango

Ave. Jalisco

C. 16 de Septiembre

Ave. Rodriguez

5

C. Hermosillo

0   1/2 mi

0   1/2 km

N

1 Museo de Cera (Wax Museum)

2 Caliente Race & Sports Book

3 Palacio de la Cultura

4 Centro Cultural Tijuana

5 Tepoznieves

6 L.A. Cetto Winery

7 Playas de Tijuana

Vibrant, chaotic, colorful, and confounding, Tijuana is Mexico's fourth largest city and just a 20-minute drive from downtown San Diego. T.J., as San Diegans call it, was little more than a village at the turn of the 20th century, but it grew explosively in response to the needs of San Diego and the rest of California, providing a workforce for factories and fields, especially during World War II. It also offered succor, becoming a decadent playground for Americans deprived of booze and gambling by Prohibition and moral reformers. Today's Tijuana, unfortunately, does not possess an attractive urban landscape—its beauty lies within its fabulous restaurants, burgeoning art and music scene, plentiful shopping opportunities, and legendary nightlife. START: **Take the Blue Line trolley to San Ysidro (it's the last stop). From the trolley, cross the street and head up the ramp that accesses the border-crossing bridge. Tijuana's shopping and nightlife district, Avenida Revolución, is a $5-taxi ride from the border, or you can walk the mile (.6km) into the tourist area. The trolley takes about 40 minutes from downtown San Diego; the one-way fare is $2.50. The last trolley to San Ysidro departs downtown around midnight (3am on Sat); the last returning trolley from San Ysidro is at 1am (2am on Sat). Unless you plan on driving farther into Mexico, it's best to park your car on the U.S. side and walk across. Taxis are cheap, plentiful, and safe in Tijuana (you will need to negotiate a price with cab drivers; the white taxis with red stripes are metered and a better deal). If you do drive, take I-5 south; purchasing Mexican auto insurance north of the border is also highly recommended.**

❶ Museo de Cera (Wax Museum).

This creepy sideshow is filled with characters from Mexican history and lore, and includes a few incongruous figures like Bill Clinton and Whoopi Goldberg. And despite her presence here, there was no kindly ranchera matriarch named Tía (aunt) Juana for whom the city was named. Tijuana derives its name from "tycuan," an indigenous word meaning "near the water," a reference to a broad, shallow river that is now little more than a trickle (except during storms) running down a concrete wash. ⏱ *30 min. 8281 Calle 1*

Caliente Race & Sports Book.

Crossing the World's Busiest International Border

U.S. citizens need a passport, passport card, or similarly secure document such as a SENTRI card (used by frequent border cross-ers) to cross the border; those 15 and under must have a birth certificate or naturalization certificate. Non-U.S. citizens will need a passport, an I-94, a multiple-entry visa, or a Resident Alien Card. For more information, check with the U.S. Department of State (☎ 202/647-5225; www.travel.state.gov) before your visit. Waits of up to 2 hours are not uncommon when crossing back to the U.S.

If you walk across to Mexico, the first structure you'll see on your left is a Visitor Information Center (☎ 664/607-3097), open daily 9am to 6pm. They have maps, safety tips, and brochures that cover the city's highlights. There's also an information booth on the east side of Avenida Revolución at Third. The Tijuana Convention & Visitors Bureau (☎ 664/684-0537; www.tijuanaonline.org) is across the street from the Centro Cultural at Paseo de los Héroes 9365, Ste. 201. It's open Monday to Friday 9am to 6pm. For English-speaking tourist assistance, dial ☎ 078 (it operates 24/7); for emer-gencies, dial ☎ 066. When calling numbers from the U.S., dial 011-52 then the 10-digit number.

English is widely spoken and dollars are accepted just about everywhere; Visa and MasterCard are accepted in many places, but never assume they will be—ask before dining or purchasing. You're permitted to bring $800 worth of purchases back across the border duty-free, including 1 liter of alcohol per person (for adults 21 and older). You can also bring back about a month's supply (50 dosages) of any medicine that requires a prescription in the U.S. In 2009, the Mexican government decriminalized possession of small amounts of drugs, including marijuana, cocaine, heroin, and LSD. This does not mean that as a visitor you can't end up in a world of trouble if you're caught holding these substances. Do yourself a favor and stay away from narcotics and those who deal them while in Mexico.

The following countries have consulate offices in Tijuana: the United States (☎ 664/622-7400), Canada (☎ 664/684-0461), and the United Kingdom (☎ 664/681-7323).

(btw. aves. Revolución and Made-ras). ☎ 664/688-2478. Admission $1. Daily 10am–6pm.

❷ Caliente Race & Sports Book. This attractive, flagstone-fronted space has all the bells and whistles of a Vegas sports book. You can bet on international sporting events including NFL, NBA, and soc-cer games; there's also electronic gaming. About a 10-minute cab ride away is Hipódromo Caliente (Caliente Racetrack), at Blv. Agua Caliente and Tapachula (☎ 664/633-7300), where there's daily greyhound racing (Mon, Wed–Fri at 7:45pm; Sat–Sun at 1pm;

Tues at 2pm and 7:45pm) and another sports book. ⏲ *At least 15 min. Ave. Revolución at Calle 4.* ☎ *664/688-3425. www.caliente.com. mx. Hours vary but usually daily 11am–midnight.*

③ ★ **Palacio de la Cultura.** Showcasing the work of local artists, this large complex is set in the Antigua Palacio Municipal, which served as a seat of government from 1921 to 1986, and is one of the area's few remaining historical buildings. This is a great side trip off touristy Revolución—adjacent are the Cathedral and Mercado el Popo, a quintessentially Mexican marketplace selling nuts, candy, and produce. ⏲ *1 hr. Calle 2 at Ave. Constitución.* ☎ *664/ 688-1721. www.imac.tijuana.gob.mx. Free admission. Hours vary but usually daily 10am–6pm.*

④ ★★ **Centro Cultural Tijuana.** A short cab ride away in the Zona Río is Tijuana's cultural icon, which opened in 1982. This ultramodern complex features a gigantic, sand-colored sphere, "La Bola," that houses an IMAX Dome Theater (some English-language films on weekends), and "El Cubo," a state-of-the-art gallery that hosts traveling exhibitions. CECUT (pronounced see-coot) also has a museum that covers the history of Tijuana and Baja, from pre-Hispanic times through the modern era (descriptions are in both Spanish and English). Music, theater, and dance performances are held in the center's acoustically excellent concert hall; there's also a cafe and a great museum bookshop. ⏲ *At least 1 hr. Paseo de los Héroes, at Ave. Independencia.* ☎ *664/687-9600. www.cecut.gob.mx. Museum admission $1.60; film and exhibition tickets $4.50 adults, $2.50 children. Tues–Sun 10am–6:30pm; extended hours for films and special events.*

In the heart of Tijuana's Zona Río fine-dining district, you'll find ⑤ ★ **Tepoznieves.** This unique ice-cream parlor serves up treats that are sure to intrigue and delight, like wine- or spirit-infused sorbets, and traditional ice creams made with everything from rose petals to prunes (and yes, chocolate, too). *Blvd. Sánchez Taboada 10737 (at Francisco Sarabia).* ☎ *664/634-6532. $1–$3.*

⑥ ★★ **L.A. Cetto Winery (Cava de Vinos).** This impressive barrel-shaped winery and visitor center provides an introduction to Mexican viniculture. The Valle de Guadalupe, a

Tijuana souvenirs.

Tijuana Safety Alert

Violence has risen dramatically in Tijuana, mostly due to the presence of organized crime—but tourists are not the targets. There is petty crime, too, so observe the same precautions as in any large city: Don't flash a lot of cash or expensive jewelry, and stick to populated areas. *Mordida,* "the bite," is also still known to occur. That's when uniformed police officers extort money in exchange for letting you off some infraction, like a traffic ticket. If you do find yourself dealing with an official, never offer a bribe—you may find yourself in much more trouble than you bargained for. And if you do meet up with corruption, you have little recourse but to comply, and then report the incident to your consulate (be sure to note the officer's name, as well as badge and patrol car numbers). You can also file complaints about police or city officials in English at www.consulmexsd.org (click on the link "Complaints About Your Trip to Tijuana"). Another option is the city of Tijuana Internal Affairs 24-hour hotline at ☎ 664/688-2810; the San Diego Police Department will take crime reports and forward them to the proper agency as well. For the latest security advisories, go to http://travel.state.gov; you can also call toll-free ☎ 888/407-4747 Monday through Friday 5am to 5pm. From Mexico, dial 001-202-501-4444 (tolls apply).

fertile region southeast of Tijuana, produces most of Mexico's wine, and many high-quality vintages are exported to Europe; most are unavailable in the United States. L.A. Cetto also sells fine tequila, brandy, olive oil, and more. ⏱ *1 hr. Ave. Cañón Johnson 2108 (at Ave. Constitución Sur).* ☎ *664/685-3031. www.cetto wines.com. Admission $2 for tour and tasting (18 and over; 17 and under are admitted free with an adult but* cannot taste the wines), $5 with souvenir wine glass. Mon–Sat 10am–5pm.*

⑦ ★★ kids **Playas de Tijuana.** This large, sandy beach is popular among families. It features a line of ramshackle restaurants on a bluff overlooking the surf—great spots for lunch and a cold beer. A stone's throw away is the bullring-by-the-sea known as Plaza Monumental; bullfighting season runs April to November (☎ 664/680-1808; www.plaza monumental.com). Perhaps the most notable thing here, though, is the imposing fence that disappears into the ocean, dividing the U.S. and Mexico. It provides a stark contrast to the laughing children splashing in the water next to it. ⏱ *At least 1 hr. About 6 miles (9.5km) west of the Zona Centro, off the scenic toll road that heads toward Rosarito and Ensenada (but before you reach the first tollbooth).* ●

Street musicians.

The
Savvy Traveler

Before You Go

Tourist Offices

Contact the **San Diego Convention & Visitors Bureau** (2215 India St., San Diego, CA 92101, mailing address only; ☎ 619/232-3101; www.sandiego.org). The *Official Visitors Planning Guide* features excellent maps and information on accommodations, activities, and attractions. SDCVB also publishes *San Diego Travel Values,* featuring discounts on hotels, restaurants, attractions, cultural and recreational activities, and tours. It's available online, too. The organization's **International Visitor Information Center** (☎ 619/236-1212; www. sandiego.org) is on the Embarcadero at 1040⅓ W. Broadway, at Harbor Drive. Daily summer hours are from 9am–5pm; for the remainder of the year it's open daily 9am–4pm. SDCVB also operates a walk-up–only facility in La Jolla at 7966 Herschel Ave., near the corner of Prospect Street. This office is open daily in summer, from 11am until 7pm (Sun 10am–6pm); from September to May the center is open daily but with more limited hours. The **San Diego Visitor Information Center** (2688 E. Mission Bay Dr.; ☎ 800/827-9188; www.infosandiego.com) is between Mission Bay and I-5, at the Clairemont Drive exit. This private facility books hotels and sells discounted admission tickets to a variety of attractions; hours are 9am to dusk. The **Coronado Visitors Center** (1100 Orange Ave.; ☎ 866/599-7242; www.coronadovisitorcenter. com) dispenses maps, newsletters, and information-packed brochures. Inside the Coronado Museum, it's open Monday through Friday 9am to 5pm, Saturday and Sunday 10am

to 5pm. The **San Diego North Convention and Visitors Bureau,** 360 N. Escondido Blvd. in Escondido (☎ 800/848-3336; www.sandiego north.com), can answer your questions about North County as well as the Anza-Borrego desert. For information about Del Mar, contact the **San Diego Coastal Chamber of Commerce,** 1104 Camino del Mar, Del Mar (☎ 858/755-4844; www. delmarchamber.org). The hours of operation vary according to volunteer staffing but usually approximate weekday business hours. The city-run website is www.delmar. ca.us. The **Solana Beach Visitor Center** is near the train station at 103 N. Cedros (☎ 858/350-6006; www.solanabeachchamber.com). The **Encinitas Visitors Center** is at 859 Second St. (corner of H St.) in downtown Encinitas (☎ 760/753-6041; www.encinitaschamber.com). The **Carlsbad Visitor Information Center,** 400 Carlsbad Village Dr. (in the old Santa Fe Depot; ☎ 800/227-5722; www.visitcarlsbad.com), has information about LEGOLAND and the Flower Fields and nursery touring. Oceanside's **California Welcome Center,** 928 N. Coast Hwy. (☎ 800/350-7873; www.visitoceanside.org), provides information on local attractions, dining, and accommodations; it also has a gift shop.

The Best Times to Go

With its coastal setting, the city of San Diego maintains a moderate climate year-round. Although the temperature can change 20°F to 30°F between day and evening, it rarely reaches a point of extreme heat or cold; daytime highs above 100°F (38°C) are unusual, and the mercury dropping below freezing can be

Previous page: Balboa Park by scooter.

AVERAGE MONTHLY TEMPERATURES (°F & °C) & RAINFALL (IN.)

	JAN	FEB	MAR	APR	MAY	JUNE
High (°F)	66	66	68	69	72	76
(°C)	18	18	18	20	20	22
Low (°F)	48	50	52	55	58	61
(°C)	8	10	11	12	14	16
Rainfall	2.2	1.6	1.9	0.8	0.2	0.1

	JULY	AUG	SEPT	OCT	NOV	DEC
High (°F)	65	77	77	74	71	66
(°C)	24	25	25	23	21	18
Low (°F)	65	66	65	60	53	49
(°C)	18	18	18	15	11	9
Rainfall	0	0.1	0.2	0.4	1.1	1.4

counted in mere hours once or twice each year. San Diego receives very little precipitation (just 10 in./103cm of rainfall in an average year); what rain does fall comes primarily between November and April. Fall and spring are great times to be here; beachgoers should note that late spring and early summer tanning sessions are often compromised by a local phenomenon called **May Gray** and **June Gloom**—a layer of low-lying clouds or fog along the coast that doesn't burn off until noon (if at all) and returns before sunset. San Diego is busiest between Memorial Day and Labor Day; if you visit in summer, expect fully booked beachfront hotels and crowded parking lots. The only slow season is from Thanksgiving to early February.

Festivals & Special Events

SPRING. Wildflowers bloom in the desert between late February and the end of March, at **Anza-Borrego Desert State Park** (☎ 760/767-4684; www.theabf.org). The peak of blooming lasts for a few weeks and timing varies from year to year, depending on the winter rainfall. **Mardi Gras in the Gaslamp**

Quarter (☎ 619/233-5227; www.gaslamp.org) is the largest Mardi Gras party on the West Coast. The celebration of "Fat Tuesday" features a Mardi Gras parade and an outdoor celebration in downtown's historic Gaslamp Quarter. The **San Diego Latino Film Festival** (☎ 619/230-1938; www.sdlatino film.com), held in mid-March, has grown to become one of the largest and most successful Latino film events in the country. More than 100 movies from throughout Latin America and the United States are shown, complemented by gala parties, seminars, a music series, and art exhibits. The **St. Patrick's Day Parade** (☎ 858/268-9111; www.stpatsparade.org) takes place the Saturday prior to March 17; it's followed by a festival in Balboa Park. The **Flower Fields at Carlsbad Ranch** (☎ 760/431-0352; www.the flowerfields.com) provide one of the most spectacular sights in North County: the yearly blossoming of a gigantic sea of bright ranunculuses during March and April. Visitors are welcome to view and tour the fields. **ArtWalk** (☎ 619/615-1090; www.missionfederalartwalk.org) is the largest art event in the San Diego/

Tijuana region, showcasing hundreds of visual and performing artists. It takes place along the streets of Little Italy in late April. Held the weekend closest to May 5, **Fiesta Cinco de Mayo** (☎ 619/291-4903; www.oldtownsandiego.com) commemorates the 1862 triumph of Mexican soldiers over the French. The festivities include a battle re-enactment, mariachi music, and margaritas galore.

SUMMER. The **Rock 'n' Roll Marathon** (☎ 800/311-1255; www.rnrmarathon.com) in early June not only offers runners a unique course through Balboa Park, downtown, and around Mission Bay, it pumps them (and spectators) up with live bands on 26 stages along the course. There is a pre-race fitness expo and post-race concert, featuring big-name talent. Annually, the biggest local event is the **San Diego County Fair** (☎ 858/793-5555; www.sdfair.com), mid-June to early July. Livestock competitions, thrill rides, flower-and-garden shows, gem and mineral exhibits, food and crafts booths, carnival games, and home arts exhibits dominate the event. There are also grandstand concerts by name performers. The **World Championship Over-the-Line Tournament** (☎ 619/688-0817; www.ombac.org) in mid-July is a San Diego original. It's a beach softball event renowned for boisterous, beer-soaked, anything-goes behavior. The **San Diego LGBT Pride Parade, Rally, and Festival** (☎ 619/297-7683; www.sdpride.org), held the third or fourth weekend in July, is one of San Diego's biggest draws. It begins Friday night with a rally in Balboa Park, reconvenes at 11am on Saturday for a parade through Hillcrest, followed by a massive 2-day festival in the park. The "turf meets the surf" in Del Mar during the **thoroughbred racing season** at the Del Mar Race Track (☎ 858/755-1141; www.dmtc.com). The ponies run mid-July to early September. Upward of 60,000 people attend America's largest comic-book convention, **Comic-Con International** (☎ 619/491-2475; www.comic-con.org), each late July. It's a long weekend of auctions, dealers, celebrities, and seminars focusing on graphic novels, fantasy, and sci-fi (**Note:** Single-day tickets sell out; preregistration is encouraged). **La Jolla Summer-Fest** (☎ 858/459-3728; www.ljms.org) is perhaps San Diego's most prestigious annual music event. It features a wide spectrum of classical and contemporary music, with guest composers and musicians ranging from the likes of Chick Corea to Yo-Yo Ma. SummerFest also offers master classes, open rehearsals, and workshops. The **U.S. Open Sandcastle Competition** (☎ 619/424-6663; www.usopensandcastle.com) is the quintessential beach event, held at Imperial Beach in early August. A parade and children's sand castle contest are on Saturday, followed by the main competition on Sunday. The late-August alternative music festival **Street Scene** (www.street-scene.com) bounced around town for several years but is back on the streets of downtown where it began. It's looking to regain the luster it had in years past as one of the country's top music fests.

FALL. The country's largest rough-water swimming competition, the **La Jolla Rough Water Swim** (☎ 858/456-2100; www.ljrws.com) began in 1916. It takes place the Sunday after Labor Day at La Jolla Cove. Up in the mountain town of Julian (☎ 760/765-1857; www.julianca.com), the **fall apple harvest** from mid-September to mid-November draws big crowds. Every weekend local artisans display their wares, and there's plenty of cider and apple pie, plus entertainment and brilliant fall foliage. San Diego's acclaimed local breweries, along with guest brewers from around California and beyond, strut their stuff at the **Festival of Beer** (www.sdbeerfest.org) in mid-September. Some 150 different beers are on tap, along with food and live music. **Fleet Week** (www.fleetweeksandiego.org) is a bit of a misnomer. It's the nation's largest military appreciation event and it lasts the entire month of October. It includes Navy ship tours, a college football game, an auto race of classic speedsters, and the renowned Miramar Air Show. One of the West's most impressive celebrations of Italian culture takes place at the **Little Italy Festa** (☎ 619/233-3898; www.littleitalysd.com) in mid-October. The streets come alive with traditional food, music, and entertainment, including stickball and chalk-art street painting competitions. The **San Diego Bay Wine & Food Festival** (☎ 858/578-9463; www.worldofwineevents.com), held in mid-November, is Southern California's biggest wine and culinary event. More than 200 wineries and restaurants participate. Some two-dozen bands perform at the **San Diego Thanksgiving Dixieland Jazz Festival** (☎ 619/297-5277; www.dixielandjazzfestival.org). This annual festival is held over the long Thanksgiving weekend and features vintage jazz sounds like ragtime, swing, and, of course, pure New Orleans Dixieland.

WINTER. During the first Friday and Saturday nights of December, San Diego's fine urban park is decked out in holiday splendor for **Balboa Park December Nights** (☎ 619/239-0512; www.balboapark.org). There's a candlelight procession, caroling, entertainment, and ethnic food; park museums are all free, too. **Whale-watching season**

begins in mid-December and continues until about mid-March, as more than 20,000 Pacific gray whales make the trek from chilly Alaskan seas to the warm-water breeding lagoons of Baja California, and then back again. There are a variety of ways to witness the procession, from both land and sea (www.sandiego.org). San Diego is home to two college football bowl games: the **Holiday Bowl** (☎ 619/283-5808; www.holidaybowl.com) and the **Poinsettia Bowl** (☎ 619/285-5061; www.poinsettiabowl.net), both held in late December. The Holiday Bowl pits top teams from the Pac 10 and Big 12 Conferences; the Poinsettia Bowl pits a team from the Mountain West Conference against an at-large opponent. The Holiday Bowl features several special events, including the nation's biggest balloon parade of giant inflatable characters. The PGA Tour stop at Torrey Pines Golf Course has been an annual event since 1952, featuring the finest professional golfers in the world. Now known as the **Farmers Insurance Open** (☎ 858/886-4653; www.farmersinsuranceopen.com), it takes place in late January, attracting more than 100,000 spectators.

Useful Websites

- **www.sandiego.org** is maintained by the San Diego Convention & Visitors Bureau and includes up-to-date weather data, a calendar of events, and a hotel booking engine.

- **www.sandiegoartandsol.com** is the link for cultural tourism. You'll find a list of art shows and music events, plus intriguing touring itineraries that delve into the city's culture.

- **www.sandiegomagazine.com**, the *San Diego Magazine* website, offers feature stories and dining and events listings.

- **www.sdreader.com**, the site of the free weekly *San Diego Reader,* is a great resource for club and show listings. It has printable coupons for discount dining and other services, plus arts, eats, and entertainment critiques.

- **www.signonsandiego.com** is the *San Diego Union-Tribune* site, offering headline news, plus reviews and information on restaurants, music, movies, performing arts, museums, outdoor recreation, beaches, and sports.

- **www.wheresd.com** provides information on arts, culture, special events, shopping, and dining for San Diego, Orange County, and Los Angeles. You can also make hotel reservations through the site.

- **www.voiceofsandiego.org** is an excellent online news source that offers information on what's happening in the city politically and culturally.

- **www.sezio.org** is a hip spot where you can check in with the local art and music scene and learn about the latest openings and shows.

Getting **There**

By Plane
San Diego International Airport (☎ 619/231-2100; www.san.org), also known as Lindbergh Field (airport code: SAN), is just 3 miles (4.8km) northwest of downtown San Diego. It isn't a connecting hub for domestic airlines, and most international travel arrives via Los Angeles or points east. Planes land at Terminal 1 or 2, though most flights to and from Southern California airports use the Commuter Terminal, a half-mile (.8km) away; the Airport Flyer ("red bus") provides free service from the main airport to the Commuter Terminal, or there's a footpath. General **information desks** with visitor materials, maps, and other services are near the baggage claim areas of both Terminal 1 and 2. You can exchange foreign currency at **Travelex America** (☎ 619/681-1941; www.travelex. com) in Terminal 2 on the second level (*inside* the security area, near the gates). **Hotel reservation** and **car-rental courtesy phones** are in

the baggage-claim areas of Terminal 1 and 2. Major airlines flying into San Diego include **AeroMéxico** (☎ 800/237-6639; www.aero mexico.com), **Air Canada** (☎ 888/ 247-2262; www.aircanada.com), **AirTran Airways** (☎ 800/247-8726; www.airtran.com), **Alaska Airlines/Horizon Air** (☎ 800/252-7522; www.alaskaair.com), **Allegiant Air** (☎ 702/505-8888; www. allegiantair.com), **American Airlines** (☎ 800/433-7300; www.aa. com), **Continental Airlines** (☎ 800/ 523-3273; www.continental.com), **Delta Airlines** (☎ 800/221-1212; www.delta.com), **Frontier Airlines** (☎ 800/432-1359; www.frontier airlines.com), **Hawaiian Airlines** (☎ 800/367-5320; www.hawaiian air.com), **JetBlue Airways** (☎ 800/ 538-2583; www.jetblue.com), **Southwest Airlines** (☎ 800/435-9792; www.southwest.com), **Sun Country Airlines** (☎ 800/359-6786; www.suncountry.com), **United Airlines** (☎ 800/864-8331; www.united.com), **US Airways**

(☎ 800/428-4322; www.usairways. com), **Virgin America** (☎ 877/359-8474; www.virginamerica.com), and **WestJet** (☎ 888/937-8538; www. westjet.com). The Commuter Terminal is used by regional carriers **American Eagle** and **United Express** and for connecting flights to Los Angeles (for flight info, contact the parent carriers).

By Bus & Train

Greyhound buses (☎ 800/231-2222; www.greyhound.com) from Los Angeles, Phoenix, Las Vegas, and other points in the Southwest arrive at the station in downtown San Diego at 120 W. Broadway (☎ 619/239-3266). Local buses stop in front and the San Diego Trolley line is nearby.

The **Metropolitan Transit System** (☎ 619/233-3004; www. transit.511sd.com) operates the San Diego Transit Flyer—bus route no. 992—providing service between the airport and downtown San Diego, running along Broadway. Bus stops are at each of Lindbergh Field's three terminals. The one-way fare is $2.25, and exact change is required. If you're connecting to another bus or the San Diego Trolley, you'll need to purchase a Day Pass; a 1-day pass starts at $5 and is available from the driver or online. The ride takes about 15 minutes, and buses come at 10- to 15-minute intervals.

Trains from all points in the United States and Canada will take you to Los Angeles, where you'll need to change trains for the journey to San Diego. The city's Santa Fe Station (☎ 619/239-9021) is at the west end of Broadway, on Kettner Boulevard between Pacific Highway and India Street, within walking distance of many downtown hotels and the Embarcadero. Taxis line up outside the main door, the trolley station is across the street, and a dozen local bus routes stop on Broadway or Pacific Highway. **Amtrak** (☎ 800/872-7245; www. amtrak.com) trains run between downtown Los Angeles and San Diego about 11 times daily each way. They stop in Anaheim (Disneyland), Santa Ana, San Juan Capistrano, Oceanside, and Solana Beach. Two trains per day also stop in San Clemente. The travel time from Los Angeles to San Diego is about 2 hours and 45 minutes (for comparison, driving time can be as little as 2 hr., or as much as 4 hr. during rush hour). A one-way ticket to San Diego is $30, or $44 for a reserved seat in business class.

International visitors can buy a **USA Rail Pass,** good for 15, 30, or 45 days of unlimited travel on Amtrak.

By Boat

San Diego's **B Street Cruise Ship Terminal** is at 1140 N. Harbor Dr., right at the edge of downtown (☎ 800/854-2757; www.sandiego cruiseport.com). Carnival Cruise Lines (☎ 888/227-6482; www. carnival.com) counts San Diego as a year-round home port, while several others, including Holland America Line (☎ 877/932-4259; www.holland america.com), Royal Caribbean (☎ 866/562-7625; www.royal caribbean.com), and Celebrity (☎ 800/647-2251; www.celebrity cruises.com) make seasonal stops here.

By Taxi

Taxis line up outside both terminals, and the trip to a downtown location, usually a 10-minute ride, is about $10 (plus tip); budget $20 to $25 for Coronado or Mission Beach, and about $30 to $35 for La Jolla.

By Shuttle

Several airport shuttles run regularly from the airport to points around the city; you'll see designated pickup areas outside each terminal. The fare is about $8 per person to downtown hotels; Mission Valley and Mission Beach hotels are $12; La Jolla, $20; and Coronado hotels $16. Rates to a residence are about $5–$10 more than the above rates for the first person. One company that serves all of San Diego County is **SuperShuttle** (☎ 800/974-8885; www.supershuttle.com).

By Car

If you're driving to downtown from the airport, take Harbor Drive south to Broadway, the main east–west thoroughfare, and turn left. To reach Hillcrest or Balboa Park, exit the airport toward I-5, and follow the signs for Laurel Street. To reach Mission Bay, take I-5 north to I-8 west. To reach La Jolla, take I-5 north to the La Jolla Parkway exit, bearing left onto Torrey Pines Road. Three main interstates lead into San Diego. **I-5** is the primary route from San Francisco, central California, and Los Angeles; it runs straight through downtown to the Tijuana border crossing. **I-8** cuts across California from points east like Phoenix, terminating just west of I-5 at Mission Bay. **I-15** leads from the deserts to the north through inland San Diego; as you enter Miramar, take **Hwy. 163** south to reach the central parts of the city.

Getting **Around**

By Car

Most downtown streets run one-way, in a grid pattern. However, outside downtown, canyons and bays often make streets indirect. Finding a parking space can be tricky in the Gaslamp Quarter, Old Town, Mission Beach, and La Jolla, but parking lots are often centrally located. Rush hour on the freeways is generally concentrated from 7 to 9am and 4:30 to 6pm (for up-to-the-minute traffic info, dial ☎ 511). A few things to note: San Diego's gas prices are often among the highest in the country; California has a seat-belt law for both drivers and passengers; drivers are required to use hands-free cell phone technology; text messaging while driving is illegal; and smoking in a car with a child age 17 or under is punishable by a $100 fine. You may turn right at a red light after stopping unless a sign says otherwise; likewise, you can turn left on a red light from a one-way street onto another one-way street after coming to a full stop. Penalties in California for drunk driving are among the toughest in the country; the main beach arteries (Grand, Garnet, and Mission) sometimes have random checkpoints set up to catch impaired drivers. If you plan to drive to Mexico, be sure to check with your insurance company at home to verify exactly the limits of your policy. Mexican car insurance is available—and highly recommended—from various agencies (visible to drivers heading into Mexico) on the U.S. side of the border.

All the major car-rental firms have an office at the airport and several have them in larger hotels. Some of the national companies include **Alamo** (☎ 800/462-5266; www.alamo.com), **Avis** (☎ 800/331-1212; www.avis.com), **Budget** (☎ 800/527-0700; www.budget.com), **Dollar** (☎ 800/800-4000; www.dollar.com), **Enterprise** (☎ 800/261-7331; www.enterprise.com), **Hertz** (☎ 800/654-3131; www.hertz.com), **National** (☎ 800/227-7368; www.nationalcar.com), and **Thrifty** (☎ 800/847-4389; www.thrifty.com). Some companies, including Avis, will allow their cars into Mexico as far as Ensenada, but other rental outfits won't allow you to drive south of the border.

By Bus

The **MTS Transit Store,** 102 Broadway at First Avenue (☎ 619/234-1060), dispenses passes, tokens, timetables, maps, brochures, and lost-and-found information. It issues ID cards for seniors 60 and older, and for travelers with disabilities, all of whom pay $1.10 per ride. Request a copy of the useful brochure *Fun Places by Bus & Trolley*, which details the city's most popular tourist attractions and the buses that will take you to them. The office is open Monday through Friday 9am to 5pm. Most bus fares are $2.25. Buses accept dollar bills and coins, but drivers can't give change. If you need to make a connection with another bus or trolley, purchase a $5 day pass from the driver, at the Transit Store, trolley station ticket vending machine, or online. It gives you unlimited use of most bus and trolley routes for the rest of the service day. For assistance with route information from a living, breathing entity, call ☎ 619/233-3004. You can also view timetables, maps, and fares online at www.transit.511sd.com; there is also a downloadable version of *Fun Places by Bus & Trolley*. If you know your route and just need schedule information—or automated answers to FAQs—call **Info Express** (☎ 619/685-4900) from any touch-tone phone, 24 hours a day.

By Trolley

The San Diego Trolley is great for visitors, particularly if you're staying downtown or plan to visit Tijuana. There are three routes. The **Blue Line** travels from the Mexican border (San Ysidro) north through downtown and Old Town, with some trolleys continuing into Mission Valley. The **Orange Line** runs from downtown east through Lemon Grove and El Cajon. The **Green Line** runs from Old Town through Mission Valley to Qualcomm Stadium, San Diego State University, and on to Santee. The trip to the border takes 40 minutes from downtown; from downtown to Old Town takes 10 to 15 minutes. Trolleys operate on a self-service fare-collection system; riders buy tickets from machines in stations before boarding (some machines require exact change). It's a flat fare of $2.50 for travel between any two stations; a $5 day pass is also available, good for all trolley trips and most bus routes. Fare inspectors board trains at random to check tickets. The lines run every 15 minutes during the day and every 30 minutes at night; during peak weekday rush hours the Blue Line runs every 10 minutes. There is also expanded service to accommodate events at PETCO Park and Qualcomm Stadium. Trolleys stop at each station for only 30 seconds. To open the door for boarding, push the lighted green button; to open the door to exit the trolley, push the lighted white button. For recorded transit information, call ☎ 619/685-4900. To speak with a customer service representative, call ☎ 619/233-3004 (TTY/TDD 619/234-5005), daily from 5:30am to 8:30pm. For wheelchair lift info, call ☎ 619/595-4960. The trolley generally operates daily from 5am to about midnight; the Blue Line provides limited but additional service between Old Town and San Ysidro throughout the night from Saturday evening to Sunday morning; check the website at www.transit.511sd.com for additional details.

By Train

San Diego's express rail commuter service, the **Coaster,** travels between the downtown Santa Fe Depot station and the Oceanside Transit Center, with stops at Old Town, Sorrento Valley, Solana Beach, Encinitas, and Carlsbad. Fares range from $5 to $6.50 each way, depending on how far you go, and can be paid by credit card at vending machines at each station. Eligible seniors and riders with disabilities pay $2.50 to $3.25. The scenic trip between downtown San Diego and Oceanside takes 1 hour. Trains run Monday through Friday, from about 6:30am to 7pm, with four trains in each direction on Saturday; call ☎ 800/262-7837 or log on to www.transit.511sd.com for info. The **Sprinter** rail service runs west to east alongside Hwy. 78, from Oceanside to Escondido. The Sprinter operates Monday through Friday from about 4am to 9pm daily, with service every 30 minutes in both directions. On weekends, trains run every half-hour from 9:30am to 5:30pm (westbound) and 10:30am to 6:30pm (eastbound). There is hourly service before and after those times. Basic one-way fare is $2; $1 for seniors and travelers with disabilities.

By Taxi

Rates are based on mileage and can add up quickly in sprawling San Diego—a trip from downtown to La Jolla will cost about $30 to $35. Other than in the Gaslamp Quarter after dark, taxis don't cruise the streets as they do in other cities, so you have to call ahead for quick pickup. Among the local companies are **Orange Cab** (☎ 619/291-3333), **San Diego Cab** (☎ 619/226-8294), and **Yellow Cab** (☎ 619/234-6161). The **Coronado Cab Company** (☎ 619/435-6211) serves Coronado.

By Ferry & Water Taxi

There's regularly scheduled ferry service between San Diego and Coronado (☎ 800/442-7847; www.sdhe.com for information). Ferries leave from the Broadway Pier (1050 N. Harbor Dr., at the intersection with Broadway) and the Fifth Avenue Landing (600 Convention Way, behind the Convention Center). Broadway Pier departures are scheduled Sunday through Thursday on the hour from 9am to 9pm, and Friday and Saturday until 10pm. They return from the Ferry Landing in Coronado to the Broadway Pier Sunday through Thursday every hour on the half-hour from 9:30am to 9:30pm and Friday and Saturday until 10:30pm. Trips from the Convention Center depart about every 2 hours beginning at 9:25am, with the final departure at 8:25pm (10:25pm Fri–Sat); return trips begin at 9:17am, then run about every 2 hours thereafter until 8:17pm (10:17pm Fri–Sat). The ride takes 15 minutes. The fare is $3.50 each way; buy tickets at the San Diego Harbor Excursion kiosk on Broadway Pier, the Fifth Avenue Landing, or at the Ferry Landing in Coronado. **Note:** The ferries do not accommodate cars.

Water taxis (☎ 619/235-8294; www.sdhe.com) will pick you up from any dock around San Diego Bay and operate Sunday through Thursday from 9:30am to 8pm, and Friday and Saturday 9:30am to 10pm, with extended hours in summer. If you're staying in a downtown hotel, this is a great way to get to Coronado. Boats are sometimes available at the spur of the moment, but reservations are advised. Fares are $7 per person to most locations.

By Bicycle

San Diego is ideal for exploration by bicycle, and many roads have designated bike lanes. Bikes are available for rent in most areas. San Diego Ridelink publishes a comprehensive map of the county detailing bike *paths* (for exclusive use by bicyclists), bike *lanes* (alongside motor vehicle ways), and bike *routes* (shared ways designated only by bike-symbol signs). The free San Diego Region Bike Map is available online at www.511sd.com, or by calling ☎ 619/699-1900; it can also be found at visitor centers. **The San Diego County Bicycle Coalition** (☎ 858/487-6063; www.sdcbc.org) is also a great resource.

Fast **Facts**

AREA CODES   San Diego's main area code is **619,** used primarily by downtown, uptown, Mission Valley, Point Loma, Coronado, La Mesa, El Cajon, and Chula Vista. The area code **858** is used for northern and coastal areas, including Mission Beach, Pacific Beach, La Jolla, Del Mar, Rancho Santa Fe, and Rancho Bernardo. Use **760** to reach the remainder of San Diego County, including Encinitas, Carlsbad, Oceanside, Escondido, Ramona, Julian, and Anza-Borrego.

ATMs & BANKS   One of California's most popular banks is Wells Fargo, a member of the Star, PLUS, and Interlink systems. It has hundreds of ATMs at branches and stores (including most Vons supermarkets) throughout San Diego County. Another statewide bank is Bank of America, which accepts PLUS, Star, Cirrus, and Interlink cards. Banks are open weekdays, 9am to 4pm or later, and sometimes Saturday morning.

BABYSITTERS   **Marion's Childcare** (☎ 888/891-5029; www.hotelchildcare.com) has bonded babysitters available to come to your hotel room; rates start at $17 per hour with a 4-hour minimum. **Panda's Domestic Service Agency** (☎ 619/295-3800; www.sandiegobabysitters.com) is also available.

B&BS   Check with the **San Diego Bed & Breakfast Guild** (☎ 800/619-7666; www.bandbguildsandiego.org).

BEACH & WEATHER REPORT   Call ☎ 619/221-8824. You can also check www.sandiego.gov/lifeguards/beaches for descriptions and water quality info.

CONSULATES & EMBASSIES   All embassies are in the nation's capital, Washington, D.C. Some consulates are in major U.S. cities, and most nations have a mission to the United Nations in New York City. For addresses and phone numbers of embassies in Washington, D.C., call ☎ 202/555-1212 or log on to www.embassy.org/embassies. The **British Consulate** in San Diego is at 7979 Ivanhoe Ave., La Jolla CA 92037 (☎ 858/353-3633). The **Mexican Consulate** is at 1549 India St., San Diego, CA 92101 (☎ 619/231-8414).

DENTISTS   For dental referrals, contact the San Diego County Dental Society at ☎ 800/201-0244 (www.sdcds.org), or call ☎ **800/DENTIST** (www.1800dentist.com).

TRAVELERS WITH DISABILITIES   **Accessible San Diego** (☎ 619/325-7550; www.asd.travel) has an info line that helps travelers find accessible hotels, tours, attractions, and transportation. The annual *Access in San Diego* pamphlet, a citywide guide with specifics on which establishments are accessible for those with visual, mobility, or hearing disabilities can be ordered online for $7.50; a downloadable version can be purchased for $5. Manual wheelchairs with balloon tires are available free of charge daily at the main lifeguard stations in Ocean Beach, Mission Beach, Pacific Beach, La Jolla, and Del Mar, among others. Beach conditions permitting, the Mission Beach, Coronado, and Oceanside lifeguard stations also have electric wheelchairs available. Mission Beach hours are daily (except Tues) 11:30am to 4:30pm from May through October, and Friday to Sunday, 11:30am to 3:30pm, from November through April (☎ 619/525-8247); for Coronado information call ☎ 619/435-0126, Del Mar ☎ 858/755-1556, Oceanside ☎ 760/435-4018. Airport transportation for travelers with disabilities is available in vans holding one or two wheelchairs from **SuperShuttle** (☎ 800/974-8885, TDD 866/472-4497; www.super shuttle.com).

DOCTORS For a doctor referral, contact the **San Diego County Medical Society** (☎ 858/565-8888; www.sdcms.org) or **Scripps Health** (☎ 800/727-4777; www. scripps.org).

ELECTRICITY Like Canada, the United States uses 110–120 volts AC (60 cycles), compared to 220–240 volts AC (50 cycles) in most of Europe, Australia, and New Zealand. Downward converters that change 220–240 volts to 110–120 volts can be difficult to find in the United States, so bring one with you.

EMERGENCIES Call ☎ 911 for fire, police, or ambulance. The main police station is at 1401 Broadway, at 14th Street (☎ 619/531-2000, or TTY/TDD 619/233-3323). If you encounter serious problems, contact the San Diego chapter of **Traveler's Aid International** at ☎ 619/295-8393, or log on to

www.travelersaid.org to help direct you to a local branch. This nationwide, nonprofit, social-service organization is geared to helping travelers in difficult straits, including reuniting families separated while traveling, providing food and/or shelter to people stranded without cash, or emotional counseling.

HOSPITALS Near downtown San Diego, **UCSD Medical Center–Hillcrest** (200 W. Arbor Dr.; ☎ 619/543-6222; health.ucsd.edu) has the most convenient emergency room. In La Jolla, **UCSD Thornton Hospital** (9300 Campus Point Dr.; ☎ 858/657-7000; health.ucsd.edu) has a good emergency room, and you'll find another in Coronado, at **Sharp Coronado Hospital** (250 Prospect Place, opposite the Marriott Resort; ☎ 619/522-3600; www.sharp.com).

HOT LINES AIDS/STD/Hepatitis Hotline (☎ 800/367-2437); Alcoholics Anonymous (☎ 619/265-8762); Debtors Anonymous (☎ 619/525-3065); Mental Health referral and Suicide Crisis Line (☎ 800/479-3339); or Traveler's Aid Society (☎ 619/295-8393).

INSURANCE/LOST LUGGAGE On flights within the U.S., checked baggage is covered up to $3,300 per ticketed passenger. Liability limits vary for international travel; check with your carrier for specifics. If you plan to check items more valuable than what's covered by the standard liability, see if your homeowner's policy covers your valuables or get baggage insurance as part of a comprehensive travel-insurance package. If your luggage is lost, immediately file a lost-luggage claim at the airport, detailing the luggage contents. Most airlines require that you report delayed, damaged, or lost baggage within 24 hours of arrival. The airlines are required to deliver luggage, once they have found it, directly to your house or destination free of charge.

INSURANCE/MEDICAL Unlike many European countries, the United States does not usually offer free or low-cost medical care to its citizens or visitors. Doctors and hospitals are expensive, and in most cases will require advance payment or proof of coverage before they render their services. Good policies will cover the cost of an accident, repatriation, or death. Packages, such as **Europ Assistance's Worldwide Healthcare Plan,** are sold by European automobile clubs and travel agencies at attractive rates; you can contact **Europ Assistance USA** at ☎ 240/330-1000 (www.worldwide assistance.com). Though lack of health insurance may prevent you from being admitted to a hospital in nonemergencies, don't worry about being left on a street corner to die: The American way is to fix you now and bill the living daylights out of you later.

INSURANCE FOR BRITISH TRAVELERS Most big travel agents offer their own insurance and will probably try to sell you their package when you book a holiday. Think before you sign. **Britain's Consumers' Association** recommends that you insist on seeing the policy and reading the fine print before buying travel insurance. **The Association of British Insurers** (☎ 020/7600-3333; www.abi.org.uk) can provide advice; you might also shop around for better deals: Try **Columbus Direct** (☎ 0870/033-9988; www.columbusdirect.net).

INSURANCE FOR CANADIAN TRAVELERS Canadians should check with their provincial health plan offices or call **Health Canada** (☎ 866/225-0709; www.hc-sc.gc.ca) to find out the extent of their coverage and what documentation and receipts they must take home in case they are treated in the United States.

INSURANCE/TRIP CANCELLATION This will help retrieve your money if you have to back out of a trip or depart early, or if your travel supplier goes bankrupt. Permissible reasons for trip cancellation can range from sickness to natural disasters to the State Department declaring a destination unsafe for travel. For more information, contact one of the following recommended insurers: **Access America** (☎ 800/284-8300; www.accessamerica.com), **MH Ross Travel Insurance Services** (☎ 800/423-3632; www.mhross.com), **Travel Guard International** (☎ 800/826-4919; www.travelguard.com), **Travel Insured International** (☎ 800/243-3174; www.travelinsured.com), and **Travelex Insurance Services** (☎ 800/228-9792; www.travelex-insurance.com).

INTERNET If you have your laptop, cafes, coffeehouses, and hotels provide a multitude of wireless options. For those without a computer, you can find terminals at all **public libraries,** including the downtown central library (820 E St., ☎ 619/236-5800; www.sandiego.gov); the Pacific Beach branch (4275 Cass St., ☎ 858/581-9934); and La Jolla (7555 Draper Ave., ☎ 858/552-1657). Another option is **Lestat's Coffee House,** 3343 Adams Ave., Normal Heights (☎ 619/291-4043; www.lestats.com), which is open 24 hours.

LIQUOR LAWS The legal age for purchase and consumption of alcoholic beverages in California is 21. Proof of age is a necessity—it's often requested at bars, nightclubs, and restaurants, even from those well into their 30s and 40s, so always bring ID when you go out. Beer, wine, and hard liquor are sold daily from 6am–2am and are available in grocery stores. Do not carry open containers of alcohol in your car or any public area that isn't zoned for alcohol consumption—the police can fine you on the spot. **Alcohol is forbidden at all city beaches, boardwalks, and coastal parks.** Pay heed or pay the price: First-time violators face a $250 fine.

MAIL   At press time, domestic postage rates are 28¢ for a postcard and 44¢ for a letter. For international mail, a first-class letter of up to 1 ounce costs 98¢ (75¢ to Canada and Mexico); a first-class postcard costs the same as a letter. For more information go to www.usps.com and click on "Calculate Postage."

San Diego's main post office is in the boondocks, but the former main office, just west of Old Town at 2535 Midway Dr., is a good alternative; it's open Monday from 7am to 5pm, Tuesday through Friday from 8am to 5pm, and Saturday from 8am to 4pm. Downtown post offices are at 815 E St. (Mon–Fri 10am–5pm) and at 51 Horton Plaza, next to the Westin Hotel (Mon–Fri 9:30am–6pm, Sat 10am–5pm). Additionally, a post office is in the Mission Valley Shopping Center, next to Macy's (Mon–Fri 9:30am–6pm, Sat 9:30am–4pm). For more information, call ☎ 800/275-8777 or log onto the website.

PASSPORTS   Always keep a photocopy of your passport with you when traveling. If it's lost or stolen, having a copy facilitates the reissuing process at a local consulate or embassy. Keep your passport and other valuables in either the hotel's or room's safe.

RESTROOMS   Toilets can be found in hotel lobbies, bars, restaurants, museums, department stores, railway and bus stations, and service stations. Large hotels and fast-food restaurants are often the best bet for clean facilities. Restaurants and bars in resorts or heavily visited areas may reserve their restrooms for patrons. Horton Plaza and Seaport Village downtown, Balboa Park,

Old Town State Historic Park in Old Town, and the Ferry Landing Marketplace in Coronado all have well-marked public restrooms. In general, you won't have a problem finding one.

SAFETY   San Diego is a relatively safe destination, by big-city standards. Of the 10 largest cities in the United States, it historically has had the lowest incidence of violent crime, per capita. Virtually all areas of the city are safe during the day. In Balboa Park, caution is advised in areas not frequented by regular foot traffic (particularly off the walkways on the Sixth Avenue side of the park). Transients are common in San Diego—especially downtown, in Hillcrest, and in the beach area. They are rarely a problem, but can sometimes be unpredictable. Downtown areas to the east of PETCO Park are sparsely populated after dusk, and poorly lit. Parts of the city that are usually safe on foot at night include the Gaslamp Quarter, Hillcrest, Old Town, Mission Valley, La Jolla, and Coronado.

SMOKING   Smoking is prohibited in nearly all indoor public places, including theaters, hotel lobbies, and enclosed shopping malls. State law prohibits smoking in all restaurants and bars, except those with outdoor seating. San Diego has also banned smoking from all city beaches and parks, which includes Mission Bay Park and Balboa Park, as well as piers and boardwalks. It is also illegal to smoke in a vehicle with a child 17 or younger present; you can't be pulled over for this but an officer can tack it on to another infraction.

TAXES   Sales tax in restaurants and shops is 8.75%. Hotel tax is 10.5%, or 12.5% for properties with more than 70 rooms.

TELEPHONES   **Local calls** made from public pay phones cost either

35¢ or 50¢. Pay phones do not accept pennies, and few will take anything larger than a quarter. Most long-distance and international calls can be dialed directly from any phone. **For calls within the United States and to Canada,** dial 1 followed by the area code and the seven-digit number. **For other international calls,** dial 011 followed by the country code, city code, and the number you are calling. For **reversed-charge or collect calls,** and for person-to-person calls, dial the number 0 then the area code and number; an operator will come on the line, and you should specify whether you are calling collect, person-to-person, or both. If your operator-assisted call is international, ask for the overseas operator. For **local directory assistance** ("information"), dial 411; for long-distance information, dial 1 and then the appropriate area code and 555-1212.

TIME ZONE   San Diego, like the rest of the West Coast, is in the Pacific Standard Time zone, which is 8 hours behind Greenwich Mean Time.

Daylight saving time is observed. To check the time, call ☎ 619/853-1212.

TIPPING   In hotels, tip **bellhops** at least $1 per bag ($2–$3 if you have a lot of luggage) and tip the **chamber staff** $1 to $2 per day (more if you've left a disaster area to clean up). Tip the **doorman** or **concierge** only if he or she has provided you with some specific service (for example, calling a cab for you or obtaining difficult-to-get theater tickets). Tip the **valet-parking attendant** $1 every time you get your car. In restaurants, bars, and nightclubs, tip **service staff** 15% to 20% of the check, tip **bartenders** 10% to 15%, and tip **checkroom attendants** $1 per garment. Tip **cab drivers** 15% of the fare; tip **skycaps** at airports at least $1 per bag ($2–$3 if you have a lot of luggage); and tip **hairdressers** and **barbers** 15% to 20%.

TRANSIT INFORMATION   Call ☎ 619/233-3004 (TTY/TDD 619/234-5005), or log onto www.transit.511sd.com. If you know your bus route and just need schedule information, call ☎ 619/685-4900.

A Brief **History**

It's believed humans first arrived in San Diego's coastal areas some 20,000 years ago, while others settled in the desert about 8,000 years later. The first cultural group, which is now referred to as the San Dieguito people, date back to 7,500 BCE. They were followed by the La Jollan culture, which populated the coastal mesas until about 1,000 to 3,000 years ago. The Diegueños followed about 1,500 years ago, and existed in two groups: the Ipai, who lived along the San Diego River and northeast toward what is now Escondido, and the Tipai, or

Kumeyaay, who lived south of the river into Baja California and east toward Imperial Valley.

In 1542, a Portuguese explorer in the employ of Spain, **Juan Rodríguez Cabrillo,** set out from the west coast of Mexico, principally in search of a northwest passage that might provide an easier crossing between the Pacific Ocean and Europe. En route he landed at a place he charted as San Miguel, spending 6 days to wait out a storm and venture ashore—doing a meet-and-greet with three fearful Kumeyaay (who had heard tales of white men killing natives to the east and south)—before heading north along the coast. Although Cabrillo wrote favorably about what he saw, it would be 60 years before Europeans visited San Miguel again. When Spanish explorer Sebastián Vizcaíno sailed into the bay on the feast day of San Diego de Alcalá in 1602, he renamed it in honor of the saint. But despite Vizcaíno calling it "a port which must be the best to be found in all the South Sea," San Diego Bay was all but ignored by invaders for the next century and a half.

In 1768, Spain, fearing that Russian enclaves in Northern California might soon threaten Spanish settlements to the south, decreed the founding of colonies in Southern California. The following year, after an arduous 110-day voyage from the tip of Baja California, the *San Carlos* arrived into San Diego Bay on April 29, 1769, leading "the sacred expedition" of **Father Junipero Serra,** a priest who had been charged with the task of spreading Christianity to the indigenous people. Serra would arrive about 2 months later via an overland route.

The site for a mission was selected just above the San Diego River, on a prominent hill that offered views onto plains, mesas, marshes, and the sea. A rudimentary fort, the **Presidio de San Diego,** was established to protect the mission, the first of 21 to be built in Alta California (the first mission in Baja California was established in 1697). The local populace was initially hostile to the Spanish incursion, but the tribes were eventually subdued by the settlers' firepower. After 4 years, Father Serra requested permission to relocate the mission to Nipaguay, a site 6 miles (10km) up the valley, next to an existing village. Irrigation projects were begun, crops planted, and herds of cattle and sheep

introduced, but the cost for the Kumeyaay was high. Their culture was mostly lost; communities were shattered by foreign diseases from which they had no natural immunities; and those who defied the Spaniards or deserted the new settlements were dealt with cruelly.

In 1821, as what is now known as **Old Town** started to take shape, Mexico declared independence from Spain. California's missions were secularized; the Mexican government lost all interest in the native people and instead focused on creating sprawling rancheros. The Mexican flag flew over the Presidio, and in 1825, San Diego became the informal capital of the California territory.

The **Mexican-American War** took root in 1846, spreading west from Texas, leading to brutal battles between the Californios and invading American troops. By 1847 the Californios had surrendered, the treaty of Guadalupe-Hidalgo was signed a year later, and Mexico was paid $15 million for what became the southwestern United States. In 1848, gold was discovered near Sacramento and the **gold rush** began. In 1850, California was made the 31st state, and San Diego was established as both a city and county.

In 1850, William Heath Davis, a San Francisco financier, purchased 160 acres (65 hectares) along the bay and made plans to develop a "new town." Residents of Old Town scoffed, and despite Davis' construction of a wharf and installation of several prefabricated houses, the citizens stayed rooted at the base of the Presidio and labeled the project "Davis' Folly." But in 1867, another developer, Alonzo Horton, also saw the potential of the area and bought 960 acres (389 hectares) of bayfront land for $265. This time, people started moving into New Town, and by 1869 San Diego had a population of 3,000; a devastating fire in Old Town in 1872 proved to be the final blow for the original settlement.

In 1915, despite a competing event in San Francisco, San Diego's **Panama-California Exposition** was a fabulous success, and it spurred the development of 1,400-acre (567-hectare) **Balboa Park** into fairgrounds of lasting beauty. The barrage of publicity from the 2-year fair touted San Diego's climate and location, and helped put the city on the map.

Toward the end of the 19th century, the **U.S. Navy** began using San Diego as a home port; in 1908 the Navy sailed into the harbor with its battleship fleet and 16,000 sailors, and the War Department laid plans to dredge the bay to accommodate even larger ships. Aircraft innovator Glenn Curtiss convinced the Navy to designate $25,000 to the development of aviation, and soon after he opened a flying school at North Island, the northwestern lobe of the Coronado peninsula. World War I meant construction projects, and North Island was established as a Marine base. The Navy built a shipyard at 22nd Street in downtown, and constructed a naval training station and hospital in 1921. America's first aircraft carrier docked in San Diego in 1924.

Aviator T. Claude Ryan started Ryan Aviation to build military and civilian aircraft and equipment, and in 1927 he built *The Spirit of St. Louis* for Charles A. Lindbergh, a young airmail pilot. Only a few weeks after taking off from North Island, Lindbergh landed in Paris and was toasted as the first to fly solo across the Atlantic. In 1928, San Diego's airport was dedicated as **Lindbergh Field.**

A second world's fair, the 1935–36 **California-Pacific International Exposition,** allowed the Spanish colonial architecture in Balboa Park to be expanded, and many tourists were so enamored with what they saw, they became residents. In the decades to come, though, downtown stumbled the way many urban centers did in the 1960s and 1970s, filled after dark with the homeless and inebriated. In 1974, the **Gaslamp Quarter**—the new name for Alonzo Horton's New Town—was designated as a historic district. Little occurred to revitalize downtown at first, but a redevelopment plan was established and the first step was taken when **Seaport Village,** a waterside shopping complex at the south end of the Embarcadero, opened in the early '80s. In 1985, a $140-million shopping center next to Horton Plaza opened to raves, and San Diegans responded immediately, coming downtown to shop and dine as they hadn't in a generation. Another wave of downtown development saw the opening of the $474-million ballpark **PETCO Park** in 2004.

Today's San Diego owes much to **medical and high-tech industries**—biotechnology, pharmaceutical, and telecommunications in particular. One economic think tank declared the city to be the nation's number-one "biotech cluster," supported by a steady flow of research from academic institutions like the University of California, San Diego, the Scripps Research Institute, and the Salk Institute. The biotech industry here also provides a home base for a gaggle of science-based Nobel prize winners and is directly responsible for tens of thousands of jobs and billions of dollars in local economic impact.

Index

See also Accommodations and Restaurant indexes, below.

Photo **Credits**

p i, left: © Adam Jones / Danita Delimont.com / Alamy; p i, middle: © Russ Bishop / Alamy; p i, right: © Kevin Schafer / Getty Images; p ii, top: © Richard Cummins / Lonely Planet Images; p ii middle top: © David Olsen / Alamy; p ii, middle: © Richard Cummins / Lonely Planet Images; p ii, middle bottom: © Peter Bennett / Ambient Images Inc. / Alamy; p ii, bottom: © Brett Shoaf / Artistic Visuals; p iii, top: © Gary Conaughton; p iii, middle top: © Brett Shoaf / Artistic Visuals; p iii, middle bottom: © Peter Bennett / Ambient Images; p iii, middle bottom: Courtesy Paradise Point Resort & Spa; p iii, bottom: © Anthony Arendt / Ambient Images; p 1: © Rick Doyle / Corbis; p 3, top: © Irene Chan / drr.net; p 3, bottom: © Richard Cummins / Corbis; p 4: © Brett Shoaf / Artistic Visuals; p 5: © Brett Shoaf / Artistic Visuals; p 6, top: © Brett Shoaf / Artistic Visuals; p 6, bottom: © Richard Cummins / Lonely Planet Images; p 7: © Richard Cummins / Lonely Planet Images; p 9: © Brett Shoaf / Artistic Visuals; p 10: © AlanHaynes.com / Alamy; p 11, top: © Maresa Pryor / DanitaDelimont.com; p 11, bottom: © Gary Conaughton; p 13: © Brett Shoaf / Artistic Visuals; p 14, top: © Brett Shoaf / Artistic Visuals; p 14, bottom: © Brett Shoaf / Artistic Visuals; p 15, top: © Jerry Amster / SuperStock; p 15, bottom: © Brett Shoaf / Artistic Visuals; p 17: © Brett Shoaf / Artistic Visuals; p 18: © Brett Shoaf / Artistic Visuals; p 19: © David Olsen / Alamy; p 21, top: © Brett Shoaf / Artistic Visuals; p 21, bottom: © Craig Schwartz / courtesy The Old Globe Theatre; p 22, top: © Brett Shoaf / Artistic Visuals; p 22, bottom: © Brett Shoaf / Artistic Visuals; p 23, top: © Brett Shoaf / Artistic Visuals; p 23, bottom: © Brett Shoaf / Artistic Visuals; p 24, top: © Charlie Manz / Artistic Visuals; p 24, bottom: © Brett Shoaf / Artistic Visuals; p 25, top: © Colin Paterson / SuperStock; p 25, bottom: © Brett Shoaf / Artistic Visuals; p 26: © Brett Shoaf / Artistic Visuals; p 27, top: © Brett Shoaf / Artistic Visuals; p 27, bottom: © Thomas Shjarback / Alamy; p 29, top: © Brett Shoaf / Artistic Visuals; p 29, bottom: © Brett Shoaf / Artistic Visuals; p 30, top: © Brett Shoaf / Artistic Visuals; p 30, bottom: © Brett Shoaf / Artistic Visuals; p 32: © Brett Shoaf / Artistic Visuals; p 33: © Thomas Shjarback / Alamy; p 35: © Brett Shoaf / Artistic Visuals; p 36, top: © Brett Shoaf / Artistic Visuals; p 36, bottom: © Richard Cummins / SuperStock; p 37: © Mark E. Gibson / Ambient Images; p 38, top: © Charlie Manz / Artistic Visuals; p 38, bottom: © Brett Shoaf / Artistic Visuals; p 39: © Brett Shoaf / Artistic Visuals; p 41: Courtesy Four Seasons Resort Aviara North San Diego; p 42: © Jan Butchofsky-Houser / Corbis; p 43: © Richard Cummins / Lonely Planet Images; p 46, top: © Brett Shoaf / Artistic Visuals; p 46, bottom: © Brett Shoaf / Artistic Visuals; p 47: © Brett Shoaf / Artistic Visuals; p 48: © Brett Shoaf / Artistic Visuals; p 49: © Brett Shoaf / Artistic Visuals; p 51, top: © David Forbert / SuperStock; p 51, bottom: © Joe Sohm / Visions of America, LLC / Alamy; p 52, top: © Peter Bennett / Ambient Images; p 52, bottom: © Richard Cummins / SuperStock; p 53: © Brett Shoaf / Artistic Visuals; p 55: © Brett Shoaf / Artistic Visuals; p 56, top: © Joanne Montenegro / eStock Photo; p 56, bottom: © Lorenz Kienzle / Courtesy Museum of Contemporary Art San Diego; p 57: © Brett Shoaf / Artistic Visuals; p 59: © Philipp Scholz Rittermann / Courtesy Museum of Contemporary Art San Diego; p 60: © Brett Shoaf / Artistic Visuals; p 61: © Brett Shoaf / Artistic Visuals; p 63: © Charlie Manz / Artistic Visuals; p 64, top: © Brett Shoaf / Artistic Visuals; p 64, bottom: © Peter Bennett / Ambient Images Inc. / Alamy; p 65: © Charlie Manz / Artistic Visuals; p 67, top: © Gistimages / Alamy; p 67, bottom: © Brett Shoaf / Artistic Visuals; p 68: © Travel Pix Collection / AGE Fotostock; p 69: © Brett Shoaf / Artistic Visuals; p 75, top: © Brett Shoaf / Artistic Visuals; p 75, bottom: © Brett Shoaf / Artistic Visuals; p 76, top: © Gary Conaughton; p 76, bottom: © Gary Conaughton; p 77, top: © Brett Shoaf / Artistic Visuals; p 77, bottom: © Gary Conaughton; p 78: © Gary Conaughton; p 79: © Gary Conaughton; p 80, top: © Brett Shoaf / Artistic Visuals; p 80, bottom: © Gary Conaughton; p 81: © Brett Shoaf / Artistic Visuals; p 83: © Brett Shoaf / Artistic Visuals; p 84: © Brett Shoaf / Artistic Visuals; p 85: © Brett Shoaf / Artistic Visuals; p 86, top: © Ron Niebrugge / Alamy; p 86, bottom: © Brett Shoaf / Artistic Visuals; p 87: © Brett Shoaf / Artistic Visuals; p 89, top: © Lowell Georgia / Corbis; p 89, bottom: © Jupiterimages; p 90, top: © Brett Shoaf / Artistic Visuals; p 90, bottom: © Charlie Manz / Artistic Visuals; p 91, top: © Richard Cummins / Lonely Planet Images; p 91, bottom: © Richard Cummins / SuperStock; p 93, top: © Brett Shoaf / Artistic Visuals; p 93, bottom: © Brett Shoaf / Artistic Visuals; p 94, top: © Brett Shoaf / Artistic Visuals; p 94, bottom: © Gary Crabbe / Alamy; p 95, top: © Ron Niebrugge / Alamy; p 95, bottom: © Brett Shoaf / Artistic Visuals; p 97: © Brett Shoaf / Artistic Visuals; p 98: © Darrell Gulin / DanitaDelimont.com; p 99: © Gary Conaughton; p 105: © Gary Conaughton; p 106: © Gary Conaughton; p 107, top: © Gary Conaughton; p 107, bottom: © Gary Conaughton; p 108: © Gary Conaughton; p 109, top: © Gary Conaughton; p 109, bottom: © Gary Conaughton; p 110: © Gary Conaughton; p 111: © Gary Conaughton;